Karen Waldman has lived in Sydney, Australia, most of her life.

Her career began in the construction industry, after qualifying with Bachelor degrees in Science and Architecture. Following eight years in project management in her own company, she undertook a Master of Business Administration and moved into the public sector.

In New South Wales and Queensland, Karen held operational and corporate roles in the water and energy industries, progressing to the position of Chief Executive Officer.

She always envisioned a time when she would turn her journal writing activities into a creative writing career.

Newly retired, in the United States, her experiences provided the perfect platform to write about the adventures she shared with her beloved dog Sidnie, who had also made the journey with Karen and her husband.

Karen has two adult daughters living in New South Wales, so Australia will always remain her home.

Prior to Sidnie, Karen had three other Cocker Spaniels and has always been a dog lover, so it was only fitting for her canine companion to be the focus of her first book. She recently became mum to a Cocker Spaniel puppy, who, following Sidnie, has 'big paws to fill'.

www.karenwaldman.com

Sidnie meets Uncle Sam
Travels with my mum

Karen Waldman

This book is based on true events, but some names of people and places have been changed.

First published in Australia in 2022 by Karen Waldman
kwaldman21@gmail.com

Copyright © Karen Waldman, 2022
The moral rights of the author have been asserted.

A catalogue record for this work is available from the National Library of Australia

ISBN: 978-0-6489053-7-0 (Paperback)
ISBN: 978-0-6452373-6-8 (Ebook)

All rights reserved. Except as permitted under the *Australian Copyright Act 1968* (for example, fair dealing for the purposes of study, research, criticism or review) no part of this book may be reproduced, stored in a retrieval system, communicated or transmitted in any form or by any means without prior written permission from the author. All enquiries should be made to the author: kwaldman21@gmail.com

Produced by Broadcast Books, www.broadcastbooks.com.au
Edited by Catherine Adams of Inkslinger Editing, New York, and Bernadette Foley
Proofread by Puddingburn Publishing
Cover and text design by Matthew Oswald, Like Design
Typeset in Minion Pro 11.75/16pt by Like Design
Cover photograph by Karen Waldman
Author photograph by Stine Baska
Printed by Ingram Spark

To Mum and Dad
who gave me the best childhood a girl could have
and made sure loving a dog was part of it

Foreword

It is my pleasure to introduce my beloved blue roan English Cocker Spaniel, Sidnie, to you.

When I relocated from my Australian home to the United States for two and a half years, I couldn't imagine this American experience without Sidnie. So I uprooted him from all he knew. He endured lengthy flights that many humans would never undertake, and was thrust into foreign situations in the broadest sense of the word. All the time, he indulged me in my life's choices.

To thank him for the unconditional love he gave every day of his life, including those many months I asked so much of him on this trip, I wanted to help Sidnie share his life's story, while highlighting his experiences in the United States.

To do this I had to bestow unique qualities on Sidnie, so he could communicate with you directly. Otherwise, he could not do justice to all he saw, to all he surmised, or to all he imagined. Sidnie's observations are presented in full technicolour glory – skills not part of every dog's repertoire.

As the narrator, I defined my role as interpreter and translator on Sidnie's behalf. I aimed to be faithful to his values as I imparted his observations and shared his adventures – based on true events. At times, my values and opinions sliced through his story. I beg your indulgence at these intrusions.

I hope this account of Sidnie's experiences helps any pet owner wishing to make such a journey with their precious one. Hopefully it also gives our American hosts an understanding of the challenges Aussies face meeting Uncle Sam.

While I was writing this book, the world entered the age of Covid-19. For over eighteen months, Australian citizens were forbidden from leaving Australia unless an exemption was issued for limited and strict reasons, such as the need to assist in the Covid response or if the travel was in the national interest. While this restriction was recently lifted, this narrative has adopted a historical dimension.

In his story, the names of Sidnie's family and friends are factual. Names have been changed, however, in cases of business or commercial relationships.

Karen Waldman
17 January 2022

Contents

Part One	**Before**	
1	Broaching the Subject	3
Part Two	**The Journey**	
2	A First-class Consignment	17
Part Three	**The Arrival**	
3	My New Domain	31
Part Four	**Autumn**	
4	Freakish Fall	45
5	A Hunting We Will Go	54
6	The Tick Magnet	59
7	We Vet the Vets	62
8	Thanksgiving	70
Part Five	**Winter**	
9	The 'Choose and Cut' Experience	81
10	My Dietary Indiscretion	89
11	Sidnie's Snowshoes	95
12	School's In	99

Part Six	Spring	
13	Flowers and Fur	107
14	The Goose Family's Travails	112
15	Stags, Snakes and Snapping Turtles	115
16	Mum Institutes Precautions	118

Part Seven	Summer	
17	The A and A B and B	127
18	A Tale of Two Tails	135
19	The Pooch's P-rade	140
20	Where's Everyone Gone?	143
21	The Third Dimension	149

Part Eight	The Departure	
22	Ambassador's Reign Reined	155

Part Nine	After	
23	The Re-entry	161
24	An Aussie Horse Farm	166
25	Gentle Latter Years	169

Afterword		173
Acknowledgements		174

Part One
Before

CHAPTER 1
Broaching the Subject

Brisbane, June 2012
My stomach churned as she spoke, all those odd words piercing the air, but I had always trusted her. Why should I stop now?

Mum slipped it out as smoothly as she glided past the black-and-white cat napping in the Queensland sun on one of our early morning walks. It was around my sixth birthday and a few months short of her change-inducing sixtieth. As if she hadn't accepted the possibility herself, she repeated and embellished the terms. She wanted a willing accomplice in her decision.

'A white Christmas! Wouldn't you love a traditional northern hemisphere white Christmas, Sidnie?'

Even with our interstate move to Brisbane after my formative years in our hometown of Sydney, little had changed in the way of Christmas. Azure skies wrapped around sparkling oceans and pearl-white beaches. High temperatures and oppressive humidity smothered the elongated days.

For Mum and Dad, creatures of gastronomic habit, Christmas ordained the quintessential refreshing lunch of plump prawns and Balmain bugs from either Pyrmont Fish Market or Gambarro's in South Brisbane. They quaffed icy champagne, relaxed since Mum was on holidays from work. This familiar routine signalled all was well in my world.

Mum, short in height but large in opinion when provoked, usually spoke to me while we walked. At times it was to voice disgust at the dregs of an undigested meal on the footpath, or to instruct me to ignore an attractive morsel discarded at the foot of a tree trunk. Regularly it was to express her view on the latest political scandal or to turn 180 degrees and congratulate me on being so well toilet trained.

'Good boy, Sidnie,' accompanied most of my bodily functions, as if they required a higher order of intelligence, rather than feeling right at the time.

Every so often she revelled in the sun's warmth on her face or expressed a sadness clawing at her heart. At critical times, thoughts became words as she struggled with a more or less significant life decision. But her question, using my 'pay-attention-to-this' name, rather than her more conversational 'Treasure' or 'Precious' labels, required further explanation. From our time of near constant companionship, I knew more information would eventually follow.

In the meantime, we continued my daily highlight – our special time together walking along undulating, tree-lined Dornoch Terrace.

These outings usually proceeded in one of two ways. On work mornings, we set off at a cracking pace downhill towards the shady park that bordered the Brisbane River. Along the way, Mum often had to fend off the noisy grey-and-white Staffy that took sole ownership of the side-street short-cut we occasionally used. Mum's protective custody persisted whenever the snarling brown Bulldog spied me. In the nick of time, his owner would clamp a leash onto his collar.

I knew Mum found these circumstances nerve-wracking by the tension vibrating down her arm, but I also knew I was safe by her side. And because this was our carved-out excursion in her busy day, she tolerated these episodes in the hope the Staffy would be barricaded behind his red rose-bordered picket fence, or that the Bully would miss a morning, which he regularly did.

Alternatively, on weekend mornings such as today, an al fresco breakfast followed a more leisurely walk. By the 7am opening we were seated at a table outside West End's Gunshop Café. Dad drove from home to meet us for a family meal. I lay at Mum's feet, the aroma of ricotta hotcakes topped with crispy bacon, floating in maple syrup, or creamy scrambled eggs accompanied by garlic mushrooms, sending my tastebuds into a slather.

Thankfully I wasn't excluded. Mum poured kibble into a collapsible rubber bowl, supplementing it with a crunchy piece of Vegemite-topped toasted sourdough. Well known to the friendly wait staff, Mum and Dad's cappuccino and latte followed a freshly filled water bowl.

I loved our family camaraderie. Living as we three now did, a state away from Mum's Sydney origins and daughters, and a continent and hemisphere away from Dad's brother, sister-in-law and stepkids, they were my world. Mum was my pack leader, with Dad her able reserve.

As proof, Dad and I shared a fun game. Every morning Mum was at work, he traipsed up the road to the German bakery to buy a Danish pastry for his mid-morning snack. While he made his coffee, the goody ostensibly pushed far back on his desk, I easily managed a bite – or two. He never quite got the hang of 'out of reach!'

But back to Mum's bombshell.

Home and sated a few hours later, my long floppy ears ready to prick up at the next hint, I stretched across Mum's lap in her light-filled study. My head lolled over one side of the low-slung velvet chair while my bottom danced precariously over the other. Mum's hands intermittently hoisted my rear onto her leg or gently rubbed the black patches amidst the Berber fur along my generous back.

And thence it came – in a flood of marketing spiel not normally associated with Mum's reserved personality, though her increasingly senior professional roles had required her to adopt a more outgoing style.

'Sidnie, Dad and I are considering a move to America for a few years, where Christmas means cold and snow. Snow falls from the sky like powder, and it looks as if a fluffy white blanket has been draped on the ground and buildings.'

You see, Dad was an idiosyncrasy in Australia. He owned – and for several months a year single-handedly worked – a Christmas tree farm in north-east America. Accordingly, Mum added, 'You will love it, Sidnie. Snow layers the Christmas trees on Dad's farm, just like the icing on the pupcake you had on your birthday at Mandy's.'

My stomach knotted just like Mum's before a dental visit. Did she hear the twist as I did hers? But it wasn't the concept of 'snow' that rattled me (although birthday parties at Mandy's Day Care always aggravated my pancreatitis). 'Move' was the culprit, reminding me of my scary journey from Sydney three years earlier, when Mum's love and work took us to Brisbane.

Sydney, July 2009
My anxiety began when, at three years old on a cold winter's morning, my extroverted dogsitter, Sally, and I squeezed into her friend's car, more the size of a Tonka toy than a real vehicle.

Sally was a livewire. Her usual job was to entertain and walk me on weekday afternoons when Mum was at work. Sally always wore a smile on her open, round face – a face archetypical of the next decade's emojis – and acted like a wound-up dynamo when she talked in her lilting voice.

'Sidnie, I'm here,' she sang, rousing me from my siesta on the brown leather lounge. 'It's time to go to the park and meet your friends.'

I feigned sleep. Her announcement really meant it's time for Sally to stand around and gossip with our neighbours while I endured mandatory meetings with their canine charges. For since puppyhood, rather than mingle with my own, I relished ambling along a route heavy with intriguing smells.

But there was no stopping Sally. She blared like the football commentators on the telly. I stretched and shook. The rattle of the heart-shaped name tag on my collar did nothing to disguise my whereabouts. Eventually I could no longer procrastinate.

After trotting beside her, I sat on the kerb, awaiting the finger command she insisted upon – although Mum never caught onto the need to reinforce Sally's lessons. I darted across the road, optimistic about making a getaway from our so-called buddies, whose boring activities comprised chasing a ball or chasing each other.

I headed for secret scents at the base of the park's windswept trees and among the rabbit-warren of bushes, sniffing a wild fox that had made the eastern suburbs its home, and tracking the leftover scraps of last night's visitors. A drooping branch suggested a tall dog's message in need of further watering. I snuck towards the path, hoping for a solitary stroll. But when my leash locked onto my collar, a tug of war ensued, invariably culminating in us remaining anchored in a circle with the pack. From there, Sally maintained her reputation as hub central for all local happenings, and therein pursued a raft of rumours to their illuminating conclusion.

For the past two months, however, Sally had moved in as my babysitter while Mum led the advance party to join boyfriend Chris in muggy Brisbane. An Australian citizen for the past fifteen years, Chris's accent revealed Yankee origins. Set in his ways in his late sixties, he described himself as a bald, bowlegged codger and former cat lover.

But on that unusual day Sally crooned, 'Sidnie, you're about to have a wonderful adventure with a great surprise,' adopting the sales-pitch voice adults assume when you're about to go somewhere you wish you weren't.

As our long-haired, waxen driver waited immobile in his tiny red hatchback, Sally popped my black-sock front paws on the back seat and shoved my rear up onto it. Fortunately, I'm only a medium-sized dog, so Sally was able to hunch over and squeeze into the shell of a space next to me.

Now I've never been to the zoo. If I had, I would have recognised a cage – precisely into which Sally cajoled me when we stopped, distracting me unfairly with beef liver treats. Only the sight of my pink, nappy-sized eiderdown confirmed this contraption was meant for me. Suddenly its gate rattled shut!

I paced like a tiger in the oversize wire-mesh cell. Mouth dry, I blushed beneath my fur as I remembered the other lonely enclosure I'd been relegated to at the Spencers' in my birthplace of Bowral in the New South Wales Southern Highlands.

Sally slipped from sight as a man in patchy blue overalls heaved my cage onto a rattling trolley with a belly grunt that suggested I weighed more than my lean 14 kilos. I rolled jarringly across an expanse of glary concrete. Hoisted onto a moving slope and deposited in a claustrophobic space, I scanned the cavern, squinting as I tried to get my bearings. As I panted rapidly, my cage was shoved deeper into a plane's hold.

Outlines of large, stacked shapes were barely visible in the misty light. A low rumble shook the flooring and a firecracker-loud bang echoed as the door slammed closed, leaving me in darkness. As the growl morphed into a roar, the clapping of my heart rivalled my unrequited barks in force. I kept at it, though I knew I was alone.

When the noise abated to a muted hum, I yawned, relieving the heaviness in my ears. At last, my cage tipped and I sensed a finely tuned decrease in volume. But with shuddering thuds the sound returned to a crescendo. Finally, we clacked along solid ground until coming to a standstill.

With a sucking wheeze my ears popped, and the large door opened. A burst of light entered and moist air enveloped me like a soggy towel.

Relieved to see another man in blue overalls, I didn't know whether to bark with joy at my rescue or hide with shame at my puppyhood memories. But my angst abruptly ended as I spied Mum and Chris, soon formally to be my dad.

'Sidnielulu, here we are,' Mum called, using the name I associated with her cuddles.

Bursting from the cage, I threw myself into her arms. Had I known this jubilant welcome party was my reward for being isolated again, perhaps I could have coped with what I later learnt to be true cattle-class travel.

Brisbane, June 2012
With these memories still vivid, my emotions oscillated between separation anxiety and thoughts of euphoric reunions. I listened attentively to Mum's new angle on this plan.

'We will live on Dad's Christmas tree farm, my treasure. Many different animals roam across the enormous property, so you will have a smorgasbord of critters and tantalising smells to follow when we go for our walks.'

I searched my memory for conversations and clues as to what may have triggered this proposed revolution. 'Why turn us upside down and swap Christmas from hot to cold?' I whispered to myself.

Eventually I deduced that four distinct, yet significant events – some that had taken place even before my emergence into the world – had now converged.

The first had stirred in the wind since early 2003, when Chris appeared on the scene, and Mum and Chris began their paced and patient relationship. At that time my predecessor, Mum's darling Bobbie, also a blue roan Cocker, was still alive. Bobbie was Mum's divorce therapist as she separated from her husband, Frank. Bobbie sensed her dispirited moods and let himself be squeezed and hugged as tears fell on his head. Although he loved the tall and solid, yet gentle Frank, he never judged decisions made around him.

When, at the age of twelve, Bobbie succumbed to fits and paralysis and Mum had to end his suffering, it was one of the worst days of her life. She nestled him in her arms, his body hot with fever although he lay on the cold metal table, the aroma of antiseptic overpowering the air around them. As his body relaxed with relief, a sole tear escaped from his eye. Mum kissed his head and wept with deep, raw grief.

Chris realised that Mum without a dog was like bread without butter. When she couldn't pass a dog without embracing it and when she was ready to give her heart again, at eight weeks of age I entered her life. I had Mount Everest to live up to, but soon I became Mum's treasure, as she became mine.

Chris and Mum's relationship also strengthened. After seven years of toing and froing and driving and flying between Sydney and Brisbane, they huddled in a romantic little pizza restaurant in Yamba. Over their favourite double pepperoni and a bottle of Shiraz, they decided to get married. The wedding date was set for 2 January 2010, to be held in Brisbane, where Mum had won a new job.

Their wedding was a joyous affair. Mum worried that relatives and friends would be offended at being excluded, but a small gathering suited their private life north of the Tweed. The guest list was confined to Mum's daughters, Ilana and Abby, Ilana's fiancé Mark, Chris's stepson Pascal – the sometimes Australian arm of his five American stepchildren – Pascal's wife Sandi and, of course, yours truly.

Held in Dad's eighteenth-floor penthouse, the city's high-rise hub, an expanse of sprawling suburbs and the snake-like Brisbane River extended before us. Mum was radiant in a black-and-cream lace Dolce and Gabana dress from Harrod's, with gossamer butterflies appliqued on her neckline. Dad was handsome in his tux, capped off with a Christmas tree-patterned bow tie, a prescient gift from Mum early in their courtship.

This event triggered speculation about an eventual move to New Jersey. The contrast from highly urban to languid rural, from breaking waves to meandering canal – indeed, from sunshine to snowscape – was attractive to a couple that thrived on change in their careers. They agreed that this shift would not occur while Sapta (my, Ilana and Abby's grandmother) was still alive, and only after Mum retired.

Sapta, in her nineties, a grey-haired, roly-poly, in contrast to the svelte hour-glass of bygone years, lived in a Sydney nursing home. She had been there a while by now, since her husband Zeida had passed away, becoming frailer as congestive heart failure and dementia took their toll.

'Mum recognised me, mainly by my voice, and loved the ham roll I snuck in,' Mum told Dad on her return to Brisbane from one of her weekend visits. Sneaking a ham roll into the

Kosher facility always gave Mum and Dad a nervous chuckle – but it was amazing how Sapta asked for it every visit. They wouldn't deny her. With a wry smile, Sapta chewed the treat surreptitiously, her hands wrapped around the embargoed goods.

Sapta had her first stroke in late 2009 and another in May 2010. Able to eat only pureed food, a main joy in life was ripped from her. Mum was therefore not surprised to be called and told to rush to Sydney. She jumped on a plane, the guilt at not having spent more time with Sapta pounding in her chest.

The sensitive and gentle caregivers advised Mum it was time to let Sapta go, but she was torn between losing her mother and seeing her in peace. Yet, with Sapta semiconscious for several doubt-ridden days, Mum caressed and kissed Sapta's warm, dry forehead and whispered words of release. A tear formed in the corner of Sapta's eye and slid down her cheek. The moment was so inexplicably akin to Bobbie's farewell, Mum could almost not believe what she saw, let alone share it, fearful of being accused of minimising her mother's death.

A year after this heartbreak, the second event in our seemingly preordained move, the third followed when Dad failed his annual stress test. Urgent heart surgery was required and within two weeks, he underwent a quadruple bypass. When he was granted another gift of life, following a heart attack several years earlier, Mum and Dad resolved to seriously consider their future.

They didn't wait long for the fourth and final piece of the puzzle to fall into place. Mum's Brisbane job, to ensure water security for South East Queensland, had developed out of the drought affecting much of Australia in the early 2000s. The Queensland Government had spent billions of dollars on infrastructure to mitigate the risk of running out of water. And everyone else paid mightily for the privilege of running taps.

In January 2011, six months after Mum took up her role, the unexpected happened. Rain fell so heavily that Brisbane and much of South East Queensland flooded. Expecting the community to pay higher water prices in a time of water aplenty was not a viable government position. When in early 2012 the Liberal Nationals rode to power on the promise of lower water prices, they proposed closing Mum's organisation as part payment for the currently unnecessary drought-proofing infrastructure.

And so, with Mum's job on a slippery slope to oblivion, she and Dad determined the time as nigh. It was the moment to realise their vision of living in America.

Being the typical Libran she was, once Mum signed onto an 'on-balance' decision – it was all systems go. Following, in my view, undue haste in having a vet-certified rabies injection, I held the canine equivalent of a United States visa.

I would soon be on my way!

Part Two
The Journey

CHAPTER 2

A First-class Consignment

Sydney, October 2012

It would be so civilized if every journey resembled our trip home to Sydney from Brisbane. Instead of defying gravity in a dark, airborne cave, my sheepskin-lined bed lay nestled on the backseat of Mum's grey sedan. My pack close by, I curled up contentedly. I clutched my soft 'baby-bone' comforter in my mouth, reminiscent of the rabbit, duck or quail my English forbears would have caught.

Off we set for a two-day drive to various McDonalds – where we always stopped for water, coffee and a comfort break. We were not alone, as all Aussies head for the nearest Maccas whenever they're driving further than the pub.

We drove smoothly in companionable silence, or with a background of soft conversation. The sun streamed in the windows. According to my mum, while I slept, my ears, paws and jaw all relaxed, a pink sliver of tongue poking out of my mouth.

This positive experience proved to Mum and Dad that holidays with me were as pleasurable as when they went alone. They discussed how we would include these trips in our future 'American adventure'. Still unclear what that idiom constituted, I trusted it was purely shorthand for driving trips together now Mum was retired.

But any thrilling notion I harboured of a tranquil life driving around Australia was soon dashed. Within days of arriving back in Sydney, a wheel-less orange and blue plastic mini-RV appeared in our bedroom, with absolutely no traits to make it a desirable location in which to hang out. Yet still Mum and Dad encouraged me to sleep in this giant, albeit upmarket crate – me, with a phobia of fenced-off spaces from my last day at the Spencers', coupled with my harrowing experience in the less salubrious wire-mesh cage.

Rehearsals didn't last long. When I was shoved, more than cajoled into the oversized picnic hamper, and loaded into the back of a van one morning, Mum pulled the same Houdini-like trick on me that Sally had those three years earlier.

I barked furiously between gulps and with tears in my eyes, as we drove into an open, army-barrack style building with trestle tables lined up in rows. Set atop one, I hoped the white-coated lady was about to let me bolt out of my crate and return home post-haste – an April Fool's Day joke gone wrong. But it was not to be. She held and prodded me, inspected my gums, looked at my teeth and signed copious papers, just like when Mum had come to pick me up from the Spencers'.

A night in boarding school for strangers followed. In the morning I was reloaded into my portable home and the same van for a short drive. Transferred onto another sloping ramp, my stomach dropped with foreboding. The crate jerked up the steep incline into a dark compartment in an enormous white tube. I barked my displeasure, legs shaking, ears pricked and eyes blinking as they adjusted to the poor light.

Oblivious to my spittle projecting through the pocket-size mesh window, men in neatly pressed grey overalls, with 'United Cargo' emblazoned on their backs, shuffled me into a space opposite another crate in this huge hold. With only a dim glow coming from the massive entry, I discerned a set of yellow eyes staring at me from an equally misery-inducing prison. The familiar scent signalled I was in canine company.

The men dispensed ice into our water dishes and rapped loudly on our roofs. With a cursory, 'See you, pooches, have a good flight,' they promptly disappeared from sight, slamming the heavy door behind them.

A whoosh and change in pressure jolted the canals in my ears and bore down on my chest. As the metal beast accelerated, a deep rumble escaped like a dragon's fire somewhere below us. A ghostly stench of fuel mingled with the clammy breath of my neighbour. When I thought the noise would burst my eardrums, my 'baby-bone' toy, thoughtfully loaded into my crate with me, and the ice in my red water bucket started bouncing up and down. I barked my throat raw, ears popping and eyes watering with the strain of trying to be heard. For much of the fifteen hours of our enforced captivity, my companion joined in my labours. At times we were both too exhausted and had to stop, giving us an opportunity to comfort each other.

'What sort of dog are you and what is your name?' I asked.

'I'm a chocolate Labrador called Charlie, and this is my first time away from my family. I'm scared and sad. I had such a lovely life as their pet,' he answered courteously. 'Why are we here, and where do you think we're going?' he asked.

'I don't know exactly, but my parents said they were planning to go to America. I don't know where that is, except Christmas there is cold and white.'

Nasty jolts and tummy-tightening turbulence aborted our conversation. We set off barking again, but by the time conditions were smoother, my head spun with exhaustion. The air felt so cool that my eyelids drooped beneath my fluttering lashes. I curled into a ball and fell asleep, my soft toy clenched in my jaws. Unsurprisingly, I dreamt of my first dismal isolation in Bowral when but a wee pup of eight weeks.

Bowral, New South Wales, August 2006
When I woke that chilly but sunny Sunday, I suspected something was amiss. Lying alone, no bigger than a sneaker, on a clean yellow towel instead of among the moving black-and-white mass of my siblings, my antennae were on alert. I glimpsed my glistening all-black sister Serena. As usual she lay right next to our canine mum, Rosie, in the room that clearly signalled doggy domain by the carpet of newspapers that obscured the timber floor. Her eyes alighted frostily on mine.

Our breeder, Mrs Spencer, treated me surprisingly like a VIP. Weet-Bix, softened for slurping with puppy milk, filled my dish near to overflowing for the first time ever. Six faces angled quizzically as their tummies growled at the odd delay in the arrival of their breakfast. The low fence surrounding me kept their snouts out of my meal for once.

My ears rose as I tuned into the Spencers' one-sided

conversation. Mrs Spencer mused, 'Blu will make a wonderful pet. Since his features just aren't up to scratch, I don't doubt this is the right path for him.'

I squinted at Mr Spencer, hoping for an explanation.

Often Mr Spencer would pick each puppy up in turn, although his arthritic back creaked with these movements. Burrowed in his arms, we moseyed through the normally out-of-bounds lounge room, snuggled into his woolly jumper. His heart beat rhythmically in our ears and his soft breath warmed our fur. Pointing to the red, white and blue ribbons and the shiny purple and gold rosettes, stroking each silver trophy, he recounted the auspicious events our parents had won. Once he showed me the framed 'Certificates of Registration and Pedigree' and traced my line of heritage. I stretched tall and proud in his arms. It was now the duty of our litter to carry on this distinguished tradition.

In contrast, Mrs Spencer moved briskly and with a purposeful set to her features that signalled not to get underfoot. I felt that pressure now. At her ominous words, I observed my siblings from my lonely enclosure. They were a mix of pure black and black and white – but with more white than black. In comparison, I had more black fur, particularly around my eyes, making it hard to see where they began and my fur ended. I also had a longer body with bigger paws, which I tripped over all the time.

My difference was heightened by my isolation. The sunlight shining into the room through the large picture windows was doing nothing to calm my jangly nerves. I could still savour the warm puppy milk on my tongue, but now it was mixed with an acidy taste, as my tummy churned with worry. I shivered despite the gentle warmth as the light threw Serena's black eyes into stark relief.

Mrs Spencer piped up, 'Serena will definitely take after Rosie and her Grand Champion dad and win us more trophies and ribbons.' It felt part-mantra, part-excuse. 'It's lucky,' she continued, glancing down her nose at me and underscoring my fragile state, 'that I can oblige the Waldmans' wish for a pet so perfectly.'

Mr Spencer grunted as he often did when no comment was required, not clarifying my conundrum at all. Mrs Spencer added that they should be here soon as the trip from Sydney would be quick on a Sunday morning. I licked my mouth nervously. I looked enviously at Serena, now napping after finally being fed. Relieved that she wasn't taunting me, I relaxed my taut haunches.

Just then the doorbell sounded its piercing buzz. Serena woke and stretched in the graceful way of hers and glided over. I ran around, looking for a way out as she jumped up on the fence and almost brought it down on me. I stumbled over the now crumpled towel just as Mrs Spencer walked into the room, followed by three people I assumed to be 'the Waldmans'.

They headed directly to me, beaming and cooing in unison. 'Isn't he perfect – he looks the cuddliest puppy!'

I looked around to check if they were referring to me. Could they rescue me from my fenced-in pen? Amazingly, they did just that.

The soft, round lady with brown wavy hair picked me up and stroked my neck and back. I licked her hand. She kissed the little white diamond on my head and passed me to the young girl, whose name, I overheard, was Abby. Her beating heart gave me the same sense of peace as Mr Spencer's when he'd held me. The reticent gentleman I would later know as Dad Chris – not actually a Waldman – brought up the rear. He remained in the background, surveying this tableau. Abby, whose resemblance identified her as the lady's daughter, put me down, saying they would be back as soon as they signed some papers. A knot was forming in my tummy, clearly a precursor to a lifelong weakness, as they started to walk away.

'Don't fret,' Abby whispered, 'but imagine yourself as Sidnie until we return.'

She explained to Mrs Spencer that they wanted to call me Sidnie instead of Blu, carrying on a tradition of Cocker nomenclature since her mum was a child, her previous dogs being Blackie, Rexie and my predecessor Bobbie.

The other puppies moved in slow motion, unsure of what to do.

With the people distracted, and angry at being ignored, Serena scolded, 'You know, Blu, you really are an ugly dog, so those people are coming to take you away because you aren't good enough to be a famous show dog like us.'

How she knew this, I tried to fathom. Gradually a few of Mum Rosie's messages, coupled with Mrs Spencer's pronouncement, coalesced. Emboldened by my new-fashioned name and newfound status, I said, 'Mum Rosie told me I am a special puppy. I am destined to be very happy.'

I jumped up onto my pen to punctuate my bravado, thankful for my just-in-time and hopefully correct conclusion. I pictured a life with doting people instead of with a bunch of yappy puppies vying for Mum's attention. Serena shrunk back, and my brothers and sisters gawked in silence. I stood erect and tall before them for once.

True to their word, a few minutes later everyone returned. I was again picked up by my mum-to-be, who introduced herself as Karen, and they smiled happily. We shuffled towards the front door, with lots of 'Thanks, drive safely.' 'Lovely to meet you.' 'You too and call if you have any questions.'

My confidence suddenly evaporated, and my heart thumped at the speed with which events were unfolding. I looked back in Rosie's direction for reassurance. But as my eyes burned with tears, I saw that she was already busy tending to my siblings, without even a glance in my direction.

So, with big gulps in my throat, yet a sense of freedom fluttering in my chest, I decided there was nothing more to do than to look forward to the future she had predicted for me.

San Francisco, October 2012
Back in my flying cocoon, I awoke and recalled my current circumstances. Unfortunately, Charlie and I didn't get an opportunity to resume our conversation. With blocked ears, dry mouths and wet blankets beneath us, judging by the smell that permeated our area, I suspected we were on a descent. After an eternity of the tumultuous sound of engines reversing reverberating in our ears, suddenly there was quiet, broken only by Charlie and me barking in unison. Someone must have heard us. The door opened and light streamed in.

More men in United Cargo overalls entered the hold, moving Charlie's crate onto a ramp so quickly that we didn't even have a chance to say farewell. A fat, smiley man peered into my crate and greeted me with a 'Howdy buddy, welcome to America,' as he efficiently moved me onto the ramp next. As my crate glided down, his twin shifted me onto a small trolley. I inhaled the fresh, moist air, reminiscent of the salty smell of Sydney, and thought I'd been on a round trip, landing back where I began.

Everyone seemed very friendly, grinning at me while 'smiley two' topped up my water dish. I could only stare with exhaustion as snake-like trolleys full of suitcases rattled by. One expanse of tarmac looked much like another, but instead of a trip home to Vaucluse, more lab-coated people droned on about Customs and Security checks. Finally, following a volley of officious document stamping, a young man and his van materialised and drove me to another boarding school for strangers – but with no other classmates.

Released into a spartan pen, I hungrily ate the meal from the can that had travelled on the roof of my crate. Following a brief walk in a car park, it was 'lights out' in an office alone. Loneliness crowded in and my eyes teared with sadness. I missed Mum and realised I was far from all that I had known and from the security and safety to which I had become accustomed. Jetlag and fatigue took hold, but just as I was drifting off to sleep, I wondered what this long journey to America meant.

'Do personal attention, priority unloading, room service and a single suite mean I am business-class status?' I mused. While I could adapt to this standard of service compared to my previous domestic economy-class travel, I fretted at the forlorn journey that accompanied it.

Thankfully I didn't have to experience my solitude for too

long. The next day I discovered my visit to San Francisco was only to be this overnight west coast stop, without even a visit to Sausalito or Fisherman's Wharf.

★ ★ ★ ★

Newark, October 2012
Neither pondering frequent flyer levels nor blissful sleep were on Mum and Dad's agenda on the east coast of the States. One of the pitfalls of outsourcing a jetsetter pet's flying arrangements was not realising the itinerary was flawed. Their schedule had me arriving in Newark in the morning. Logically Mum and Dad arranged to stay at an airport hotel the night before, as Mum had just flown in from Australia. Checking my arrival time, Mum told me later in great detail, they found no flight with that number was due in the morning. A late-night call to San Francisco increased her panic.

Staccato-pitched questions hammered the hapless night-duty employee at home in her bed: 'What do you mean he's in San Francisco? What do you mean his flight doesn't leave until the morning? What do you mean he's in an office alone? Who will take him back to the airport? How can we be sure when he'll arrive?'

Dad, more rational and with greater calm, called United Cargo, raising a representative although by now it was 2.30am in Newark. Clearly not a novice to these situations, the operator confirmed there was indeed a dog with my cargo number on a flight out of San Francisco the next day. But as I was scheduled to arrive at 3.30pm instead of in the morning and since no one was going to get a wink of sleep, Dad decreed they should leave for Princeton and return to collect me the next afternoon.

'I don't want be so far away from the airport. Why don't we wait here, try to sleep and relax in the hotel till he's due?' a hysterical Mum pleaded.

'I'm going home. You are welcome to stay here or come with me,' was Dad's weary response. Any night Dad misses his sleep is by definition a very bad night. Having only arrived in the States two days earlier, he was still jetlagged and on a short fuse. Not about to face this nightmare alone, Mum left for Princeton alongside Dad at around 4am.

Unaware at the time of these east coast hijinks, I greeted my punctual chef and chauffeur, who miraculously delivered me to my correctly numbered, if not correctly timed, flight. Soon I was chalking up more frequent flyer miles.

After smoothly traversing the huge country, I was again warmly welcomed and promptly offloaded by beaming United Cargo men. I concluded – forget business class, I must actually have flown first class to receive such attentive service. Undoubtedly genuine displays of cheerfulness are in the job descriptions of airline staff who attend to elite passengers such as me. My travel-status ponderings were curtailed, however, when, with what could have been a drumroll announcing royalty's arrival, my trolley clattered into a building to the joyous sight of a pair of drained yet relieved parents surrounded by the entire United Cargo department's front-office staff.

As they clapped and whistled at our squealing reunion, the locking mechanism on my crate snapped open. I dived out and barrelled, barking, into Mum's waiting arms.

Part Three
The Arrival

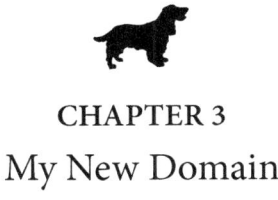

CHAPTER 3

My New Domain

Princeton, October 2012
As Dad drove, my heart pounded and I shook like a jelly. Gradually my pent-up anxiety dissipated and my muscles relaxed. I hunkered down in Mum's lap and revelled in her familiar talcum-powder scent. But my head bobbed up and down like a jack-in-the-box as I continued to check I wasn't still United's guest.

We exited Newark Liberty International Airport and headed south onto the New Jersey Turnpike, an eight-lane monster, double the size of the largest road I had seen in Australia – and that's only in one direction. Fleets of container-laden trucks rattled noisily by, wearing their own micro-climates and creating sudden gusts that scooted us sideways.

Like the speedway, cars too had been supersized. SUVs and mini-trucks outnumbered 'normal' sedans. Mum and Dad were barely holding their own in the little rented pimple amongst the peaks. We chugged along within the 65 miles-per-hour speed limit as everyone else hurtled by.

With a collective sigh of relief, we finally escaped from

the racing track onto Route 1. Dingy, unkempt strip malls brought me home to a typical Australian highway. Parramatta Road in Sydney, I discovered, was not unique. We passed petrol stations, car repair yards and mom-and-pop stores in varying degrees of disrepair. Acrid smells of fuel, smoke and dust wafted in through the vents.

Monopoly-like box-shaped warehouses and food outlets, which were greasy smelling even for me – Staples, Shop and Stop, Dunkin' Donuts – and the requisite fitness centre, such as 24 Hour Fitness, surrounded massive outdoor parking areas, oversized for a bygone, pre-online shopping era. Cars circled like vultures deciding which of the scores of spaces to take. 'Vacant' signs were slapped across smaller shop windows, chased away by bullseyes, red dots, and shiny yellow and blue.

Dad lamented, 'Target, Costco and Walmart are now national treasures.'

As well, popping up like weeds on almost every intersection, mini-shopping centres sprouted. Mum wondered despondently, 'How do all these hairdressers, ice-cream parlours, health food shops and pet outlets survive?'

Happy to hear there were lots of pet shops, I imagined we would become loyal treat-and-toy customers, just as we had with Pet Barn in Sydney.

Hard on the heels of my mirage, the pungent fumes lifted. We turned onto tree-lined roads dotted with homes atop plush lawns. Mum christened the look-alike houses 'McMansions', reminiscent of the bloated, cheek-by-jowl residences in many of Sydney's suburbs. But there the similarity ended. These were separated by grass carpets – without a fence or, strangely, a person or dog in sight. Rural scents from piles of leaves mingled with whiffs of pastoral vegetation and wildlife.

We finally turned onto the narrow and seemingly unending Fir Tree Road on which I was to live, its interlocking, half-dressed boughs shaping a welcome mantle above us. We bumped along the uneven ground and navigated oncoming cars, warily aiming to avoid falling into deep, ribbon-like ditches lining the road.

My head swivelled. The buildings chopped and changed. One microcosm paralleled our Sydney suburb, graced by double-storeyed elegance. Another comprised closely spaced, poorly maintained ranch houses. Hugging a steep, forbidding laneway, two cabins, their moss-covered roofs draped with sagging tarpaulins, were lapped by tall grasses.

Then, rounding a gentle corner, we lighted upon a field of glowing hay dancing in the breeze. Astride a belching red tractor, a large hat melted into the distance. Another bend exposed a dense forest of ramrod-straight trees ringing patchwork fields, their verdant pastures dotted with groups of grazing speckled deer.

Approaching an old stone causeway, a picturesque canal teased us with its swimming pleasures; its calm waters ventured ever closer to us on one side of Fir Tree Road. Mirroring the meandering road, it accompanied us deeper into the backblocks of this unusual setting – not quite the 'burbs' but not wholly the 'country'.

Mum proclaimed, 'On this road, Sidnie, you could bump up against rural or urban, wealth or poverty, or pristine meets neglect in a stable coexistence. It's impossible to define our little township as typically wealthy, middle class or poor.'

A little too esoteric for me; I simply wondered – with

nary a bark to be heard – where all the dogs were that the multitude of pet shops served.

We passed a tidy cream gingerbread farmhouse, the original home on Dad's property, as I later discovered, its windows framed with blue shutters, just as a comfort stop became pressing. Gravel crunched as we entered a long Christmas tree lined driveway that ended at a large barn. As the handbrake clicked, I bounded out of the car. Shooed into a fenced yard adjacent to the timber-sided structure, a gate latched closed behind me. Mission accomplished, I scurried around the grass, trees and wood piles hiding a banquet of smells. I raced around the perimeter of my own personal playpen. The spaced cedar palings prevented my escape while revealing lush lawns bordered by majestic pine trees. Between the trees, captivating avenues disappeared into endless woods.

Lured by new scents under my long, speckled nose, I thrust my snout greedily into freshly dug holes. But before I could investigate a network of tunnels, Mum realised my intention.

'Oh, no you don't – I didn't get you all the way here to lose you down a burrow,' she said, as she pushed thick logs onto the holes, to block my efforts.

Two magnificent trees formed a heavily leafed canopy above me. A refuge for squirrels, chipmunks and mice, the critters immediately scattered, taunting me with their speed and smells. I darted along each side of the square enclosure. My tail wagged dizzily.

'Sidnie, come and see where you will be living,' Mum called.

She escorted me into the expansive residence, converted from a former barn into what was clearly now a home, with grand open spaces, warm polished floors and generous, high windows and sliding doors from which I would assume the role of lookout guard. Exposed heavy wooden beams and columns delineated different levels and areas on the entry and top floors, while below, Mum told me, there was a self-contained apartment. I scurried around our section of the curious building and up and down the fluffy beige carpeted stairs. A smoky yet soothing smell emanated from two large fireplaces filled with wood and ash. Everywhere, whiffs of Mum and Dad reminded me of home.

Mum was pleased to emphasise that many of my Australian toys were already in residence. 'Look, Sidnie, Ropey [my knotted green and red rope] and Flea [my loopy, grey-green, flea-like comforter] also made the big trip here.'

Thankfully, my canned food and kibble seemed to have emigrated as well and since it was now dinnertime, Dad ensured I had a full tummy before I collapsed onto a soft oval-shaped camel bed, surrounded by matching built-in cushions. As I fell asleep, the dramatic changes conjured up dreams of my earliest adjustment to a new life, when I'd arrived from Bowral to my new home in Sydney.

Sydney, August 2006
Following my first-ever car ride, I awoke on a moist cushion of lawn. I wobbled to my feet and gazed around this pocket of sunlight. Surrounded by low stone walls, gardens stuffed with bright orange lilies, purple hydrangeas and intermittent palms bordered the grass. A checkered, brown-and-white tiled patio hugged the walls of the house. A humid, salty breeze floated around, gently stroking my fur.

I explored the springy lawn, snuffling and sneezing as I breathed in the freshly cut grass. My tummy somersaulted when I detected a canine aroma. But my fears evaporated as I delved into the moist dirt below. Another wave of delicious decay enveloped me. Discovering several particularly pungent locations, I dug as fast and as deep as my ungainly paws would go, identifying burial plots of tasty bones. My black muddy nose resembled a displaced ant's nest.

Torn between the joy of discovery and the angst of an impending confrontation, I gradually learnt the difference between these ancient smells and the new ones of my own chewy treasures. I discovered I had my predecessor Bobbie to thank for the inherited goodies.

Settled in my seaside Vaucluse home, I grew until I began to fit into my paws and fur. The rolls of wrinkly loose skin stretched to fit my tummy. Large black patches on my back became distinct, matching my ears and lower legs and travelling halfway down my tail. The rest of my body resembled a black-and-white mottled carpet.

Mum cuddled me like a baby. She rubbed my tummy, and my legs danced in the air. I licked her skin, and she pecked my head and kneaded the fur under my ears. She crooned in low, soft tones – not the authoritative voice she used when speaking in her office.

Mostly it was just Mum and me rattling around our light-filled, two-storey house. From our eastern windows, we had an uninterrupted view of the ocean to which sheer rock faces dropped sharply.

The water views were constantly shifting. Aqua sparkles during sunny weather became roiling waves during storms, but always stretching to the blue or cloudy grey skyline, dotted with brave sailing boats, majestic liners or, on Boxing Day, the convoy of yachts of the Sydney to Hobart race.

Every weekday around 6am, we made the pilgrimage northwards and upwards along the cliff roads, the majestic South Head lighthouse our glimmering beacon. Along the way we joined other parents and their charges, so that by the time the motley tribe of mutts arrived in leash-free Christison Park, we resembled a raucous exodus from Egypt. Yet no sooner had Mum bid a cheery 'Good morning' to the gathered hordes, than we were on our way downhill so she could be out of the house for work a half-hour later. While I awaited her return, I caught up on my napping – until Sally arrived for afternoon boot-camp.

On weekends, Mum worked at her dark timber desk in the study. She moved paper around or clacked away at the machine that made the same muted hum as the tall white box where my food was kept. I curled up in my wraparound lambswool bed at her feet and slept for hours, alerted to potential treats by the pantry door squeaking open in the kitchen.

Abby briefly stayed with Mum and me during my first year of life. A warm and loving big sister, she was my napping companion. Abby spent time at home resting or exercising to strengthen her knees, as they gave her a lot of pain. She also read prolifically, and as she did, I rested against her body. Was it Abby or me who had the most joy from that contact? Thankfully, following an operation, she was well enough to be able to move to my forbear's birthplace of England to study for her doctorate.

Ilana, my older big sister, visited regularly. Like Abby, she was slim with wavy brown hair inherited from Mum. She lived with her boyfriend and soon to be husband, Mark, along with their too-boisterous black Labrador, Murphy. When they married, their family grew by a medium-sized Schnauzer called Diego, but my cousins and I were not to become well acquainted until many years later.

★ ★ ★ ★

Princeton, October 2012
As my tummy rumbled, I woke from fitful sleep and wondered which meal to anticipate. Accustomed to my desires, my attentive parents promptly delivered a breakfast cup of kibble – no need for me to issue my usual hurry-up. Following a nanny-nap, I was ready for my morning walk.

I was to grow even more amazed as my domain grew substantially larger. My new home sat on 4 hectares, of which approximately three-quarters comprised grid-like rows of Christmas trees. Each tree was planted 2 metres apart, permitting Dad's mower to fit perfectly between the trees and maintain the grass at a park-like level. Trees ranged from baby seedlings all the way through to their commercial life span of thirteen years and more. Their heights stretched from my nose level, if newly planted, to towering grand old dames of eras past. With the trees of 3 to 4 metres most likely to sell, Dad could forecast how lucrative his season would be.

Bordering the Christmas tree plantation, a shallow, muddy pond and burbling creek stretched diagonally across the land. On the roadside boundary nestled the traditional Victorian farmhouse I'd glimpsed on my arrival, separated from our home by vast tracts of grass. Completing the whole, a large, covered pool sat in its own terraced backyard. How different the spaciousness was to the built-up nature of our Sydney neighbourhood!

Yet, one inhabitant of the farmhouse, completing the family of four who rented it from Dad – an aging black Rottweiler – rekindled cringe-worthy memories of Vaucluse dog-park afternoons with Sally. Mum and Dad initially thought we might become BFFs. But Morgan's overbearing nature and incessant sniffing of my privates provoked me instead.

'Leave me alone, you big bear,' I snarled, at which she proceeded to snarl back – with size on her side.

'I'll do what I like,' she said, 'and by the way, unlike you, I don't need to wear a leash. I can wander wherever I want, so don't give me any nonsense.'

As my tail fell and my nose itched with her heavy scent, I could see she was right. There was no leash attaching her to her parents. With head held high, she lumbered off. I watched warily from under my long eyelashes and noticed that her rotund figure and a slight limp hampered her agility and speed. Even so, I would have to be on my guard against her size and girth. Mum arrived at the same conclusion and decided to limit contact between us.

Mum and I embraced a pattern of two walks a day in the Christmas tree fields, crossing the narrow creek by either raft-like planks or a newer solid cedar bridge. As Mum had promised, I was indeed enticed by the critters and their smells. For, either living on our land or using it as a thoroughfare, were herds of spindly beige and white deer, cautious furry groundhogs, scurrying grey squirrels and chipmunks, and enticing white or brown rabbits and field mice.

Large, dark wild turkeys akin to the 'Road Runner' cartoons of Mum's youth appeared in the distance. So did the ugly sly brown foxes. Cunning coyotes remained invisible – though certainly audible – and while many a tale was told of the odd brown bear venturing from nearby ranges for sustenance, we never met one, luckily. The only ominous wildlife were the black turkey buzzards, who glided on wind gusts or perched in the trees, peering lustily at their next meal whenever an animal had been hit by a car or fallen victim to a predator.

At that time in early fall, the leaves glowed as sunlight bounced off the trees' orange and brown speckled limbs. Soon the red and yellow leaves turned, via a range of mauves, into a brown blanket, increasing in depth and crunch day by day. As the wind picked up, the leaves blew far and wide, eventually fluttering into mounds. With our approach sounding like a percussion band as we strode through on the leafy carpet, the deer scooted off, white tails bobbing. The squirrels and chipmunks hid in the trees and the groundhogs skittered into the nearest tunnel. And while their scents persisted, I had to be content with just the possibilities they invoked.

Some mornings following a night of refreshing rains, the dawn broke with blue skies, cottonwool clouds and a cool chill that reminded me of Bowral. My heart felt leaden as I remembered nestling against Rosie for warmth. But once Mum and I went for our walk, the weight lifted. Fresh scents teased as the cleansing rains attracted wildlife back to blades of moist grass peeping through springy beds of leaves.

My efforts redoubled to source these wonderful smells.

I galloped between bushes, under trees and along paths, dragging a screaming Mum behind. So treacherous was the uneven ground dotted with stumps of Christmas trees past, that Mum soon found a long, gnarled branch for support. But Dad, being a proficient online shopper with a penchant for multiple safety-net purchases, procured three walking sticks for her. With lights and height adjustments and stock-like tips for snow, she was now a high-tech trail blazer.

And just when she thought herself safe, I headed waterside to inspect our aquatic neighbours, who wove among the long green reeds, fertilised and multiplied by the gardening practices of the surrounding properties. We boasted flocks of ducks and larger Canadian geese, graceful blue herons and white egrets, and clunky turtles and schools of fish that somehow survived in and around the pond's shifting ecosystem.

At night I fell asleep dreaming of my day's adventures. My nose twitched and grunts of pleasure escaped from my mouth as I stretched out on one of my many oversize beds, so emblematic of this vast new land to which I'd now arrived.

Part Four
Autumn

CHAPTER 4

Freakish Fall

Princeton from October 2012
Americans celebrate their seasons with zeal. As if Broadway had come to town, lavish decorations adorned homes, reflecting the American 'out there' outlook ever on parade.

Mum and I admired the beautifications during alternative walks in the neighbouring villages of Kingston and Rocky Hill, where historic, two-tone, detached weatherboard dwellings, barely larger than cabins, abutted uneven footpaths. Aiming to outstrip each other's palette, shutters waved orange, red or mauve, against a sea of walls washed grey, pale green or blue.

Along the tree-lined avenues, complementing nature's autumn hues, wreaths were the season's feature of choice. Thatched with woven brown boughs or threaded with red, mauve or gold plants, they ornamented doors, windows, gates and fences. Metaphorically, interlocked leaves in sherbet hues of pastel pink, light blue or lemon yellow looked good enough to lick.

Not to be outdone, mounds of chrysanthemums – 'mums – peppered sloping narrow timber front decks in burnt clay or ceramic pots. Confetti buds grounded mailbox posts. As the days shortened, the rainbow splashes of these flowers contrasted with the fading foliage.

My own 'mom' (to be culturally correct, but a spelling I cannot sanction), a new settler confounded by distinct seasons, was keen to adopt the local ways. Against the barn's red cedar walls, she flaunted nail-polish crimson, pale pink, frosty white and daisy yellow 'mums in large terracotta pots, each spaced a suitable distance apart to prevent a collision when I bounded out my doggie door to chase a shy darting squirrel gathering its winter store of nuts.

Getting to know our community, it became clear that national holidays were always occasions for various 'in your face' embellishments. Thanksgiving, Christmas, St Patrick's Day, Easter, Halloween – each came with its own festoons, including pumpkins, witches, spider webs, shamrocks, bunnies or nativity scenes – with the *pièce de résistance*, the dazzling array of flashing, twinkling Christmas lights that bedecked every second house.

On a daily basis, patient souls regassed and righted plastic toothless witches and roof-high black cats; at Christmas, their reindeer and fat Santas. But come the next frosty night, these adornments shrivelled and fell to the ground. They beckoned to me at first, disguised as multicoloured bags of trash – but alas, I found no pleasure, what with their zero aroma-appeal.

Heralding Christmas, a new tsunami of wreaths appeared. At eye level, and sometimes within leg-lifting reach, my interest was piqued. Anywhere up to 2 metres wide, they varied from lush leaves with garlands of silver or gold tinsel, to cranberry bunches, or red velvet bows threaded through green fronds. Hand in hand with displays on houses and throughout the community were the allegiances to country.

If I sauntered towards a flagpole, Mum remonstrated, 'Sidnie, the American flag is flying high above your nose. I know it's peculiar to see a flag flying outside houses, but here it's *de rigeur* – so you must show respect!'

I accepted her argument, but judging by the attractive aroma percolating around the base, not all of my colleagues were similarly counselled.

Honouring those who served their nation in war, Memorial and Veterans' Days were akin to Australia's remembrance days. These days pleasurably brought me back to Oz, the solemnity of the occasion giving way to raucous barbeques and the delicious smell of 'snags on the barbie' – my kind of celebration.

Mum relished any opportunity to understand cultural similarities and differences between Australia and the US. Married to a Princetonian, she was able to attend courses at the university. Immediately she enrolled in 'American Studies' where she could pursue topics such as American values, legislation, regulation and even art, on which she then spewed forth 'educated' commentary. As her sidekick, I was destined to be the chief receptacle for her high-brow compliments and critiques – so I listened and tried to learn.

Earning Mum's sharpest criticism was the 'raw political polarisation'. As it was almost 2012 Election time when we arrived in the States, when we walked past campaign signs, she remonstrated, 'Gulfs as wide as the oceans exist between Republicans and Democrats on the economy, trade, debt, civil rights, immigration, gun control, health care, abortion rights and the environment – that is, pretty much on everything.'

I began to look for coastlines and oceans everywhere.

A comparison Mum drummed into hapless American visitors and me as an innocent bystander so often that I could parrot her comments verbatim, was: 'Divisiveness on this scale is rare in Australia. The main parties agree on much, though dress it up differently. Try dismantling universal health care or removing gun control and any party would be dead. Extremes exist, but the main parties gravitate towards the centre.'

Hungry for more fodder, Mum threw herself into the Princeton program. She enrolled in one subject per term, commencing with any course that might enhance her understanding of the American psyche, such as American Politics and American Foreign Relations. Dad also took courses, as he'd done on his previous regular trips to the States, with his preferred subjects being the less confrontational American history and architecture.

I'm not certain if it was the courses themselves that attracted Mum and Dad, or the activities they wrapped around these sessions. Mum ensured each lecture was preceded by a visit to Small World café, where she claimed the best double-shot espresso in Princeton was made – always complemented with a fruit scone to see her through the hour. Following their lectures, it was on to Ajihei for fresh tuna and salmon sashimi and prawn and avocado sushi rolls, or to the famed hamburger joint – the Alchemist and Barrister – where they each had a burger with blue cheese and bacon and a side of fries.

Meanwhile, yours truly stayed home awaiting a mingy serving of kibble that might follow their return.

Mum discovered a course led by the Australian moral philosopher Peter Singer AC, a Professor in Public Ethics at the University of Melbourne and a Professor of Bioethics at Princeton. She promptly enrolled in this class covering ethics, animal liberation and climate change. Professor Singer ably demonstrated the dire impact of global emissions. But the existence and impact of climate change – and particularly the degree to which it can be linked to human behaviour or to unusual weather occurrences – was an area of deep division in America.

This subject quickly became very near and dear to our hearts. Within weeks of our arrival, 'Superstorm Sandy', beginning as a hurricane, barrelled up the Atlantic Coast. The extremely handsome Lee Goldberg, chief meteorologist of Channel 7's New York News, forecast flooding and devastation for millions should the storm turn back towards the east.

Of course, it turned!

Fierce gales buffeted the strongest of our Christmas greens. The barn's high external walls squeaked and shook. Wind whistled through the leaky structure, returning just when I thought it had moved on. The worst gusts arrived as we settled down for the night, several hours after we had lost power. We could only imagine the damage being wrought around us, but with no light, we crawled into our respective beds to await the morning. Our home trembled.

Mum sat up stonily, ready to sound the alarm if a swift escape was necessary. Reluctant to make a move, she later told me, she imagined any twitch could topple a precarious situation. I was also on high alert, ears pricked and muscles taut. Deciding we were in fate's hands, Dad snored away, unaware of his sentries' insomnia.

I could only think back to one other natural disaster we had experienced firsthand – the terrible flooding in Brisbane in early 2011 that had sealed our move to the States.

Brisbane, January 2011
Mum's work in hotter Brisbane brought home to her – in a way that living in more temperate Sydney all her life hadn't – the reality that Australia is a paradox. Dorothea Mackeller's 1904 poem, 'I Love a Sunburnt Country' famously encapsulates Australia, and I must read it again soon.

As Robin C. van den Honert and John McAneney said in their article 'The 2011 Brisbane Floods: Causes, Impacts and Implications': 'Brisbane City experienced a major flood from 10am on Wednesday 12th January until 6pm on Thursday 13th January, a period of 32 hours [that]…spanned three high tides…More than 15,000 properties were inundated in metropolitan Brisbane and some 3,600 homes evacuated… Altogether over 200,000 people were affected.'

When Mum finished work on Tuesday night, one of the last two people to leave her office, the situation was already dire. Dad worried whether she would make it home before the roads closed. Thankfully, she passed through the streets in the nick of time. Her office building, one of thousands affected by rising floodwaters, was then inaccessible for many weeks to come.

Hearing Mum relate facets of her job as CEO of the Queensland Water Commission, with responsibility for

Brisbane's water security, Dad and I understood that the source of the city's water supply, Wivenhoe Dam, was built upstream of Brisbane, following the worst flood in Brisbane's history, thereby giving it the schizophrenic responsibility of both flood mitigation and water supply. Water releases, necessary to protect the dam's structural integrity, led to concerns about exacerbating the dire situation. The state government subsequently established a Commission of Inquiry, which Mum was required to attend. But as the Final Report stated, 'Even a large dam such as Wivenhoe has a limited flood mitigation capacity when the volume of water entering it is significantly larger than its storage capacity.'

The weekend following the peaking of the Brisbane River, as the *Brisbane Times* reported, 'about 25,000 volunteers dubbed the "Mud Army" rolled up their sleeves and lent a hand to relative strangers across the city to get back on their feet again.' Out of calamity came camaraderie.

A calamity was developing in the United States. Would the camaraderie follow?

★ ★ ★ ★

Princeton, October 2012
On the frightening night of Monday, 30 October 2012, we again survived nature's fury. Daylight revealed eight massive trees downed. Three giants had fallen in the front lawn, thankfully not within striking distance of the house. The extensive root systems of two trees, weakened by proximity to the pond, shot their tendrils to the sky. And abutting Fir Tree Road, three more fallen monsters had toppled six firs in their wake, eliminating Dad's beloved road screening.

For the next six days we had no power. We woke with the light and went to sleep with the dark. We relied on our fireplaces for heat and cooking. I snuggled close to the fire or sat on Mum's lap for warmth. I thought I often heard Mum mumbling, 'What the heck are we doing here?'

This sentiment crossed my own mind as we eked out basic needs. Creative solutions to Maslow's Hierarchy emerged.

On the all-critical food front, my meals came out of a packet (dry) or a can (wet). My 'wet' food, however, had to be kept refrigerated. Our dear friends Bettie and Fred, living diagonally across the road from us, had also lost power. But their next-door neighbours generously hooked up their generator to power Bettie and Fred's fridge. In exchange for refrigerating our food, Mum and Dad cooked for them using a grill in our fireplace.

Bettie and Fred represented all that was good in America. Original Mainers, they were straightforward and even blunt, but not terribly adventurous on the culinary spectrum. Chicken, game and steak was their normal fare, Italian cuisine being only a recent addition.

One night the mouth-watering smell of lamb chops wafted through our house. A good, ol' nostalgia stirred in my soul. Most Aussies are brought up on lamb. Mum said she'd had innumerable childhood dinners at her aunt's where the menu never varied – grilled lamb cutlets and fried potato chips – homemade sliced and diced potatoes dropped into spluttering oil. Mum assumed Americans were like Aussies, even if Bettie and Fred informed them lamb for dinner was a novel idea.

'How did you enjoy it?' Mum politely asked the next day.

To her horror, as only an honest Mainer could answer, she

was brusquely told never to serve chops again. What a waste! There was certainly someone who would have appreciated them – and Mum wouldn't have had to waste her breath asking for a Menulog rating.

The other dire consideration was our water supply. Relying on a well, we had no running water without power. Dad purchased bottled water for our drinking needs. But for dish washing and toilet flushing, another neighbourly insider-trading arrangement was planned with College Professor Jim, who lived in the apartment downstairs. Jim would refill our bottles from his workplace in exchange for petrol from Dad's tank on the property, if needed.

Finally, after six long days, the large laundry clock's second-hand moved. We realised the quiet hum was indeed a refrigerator returned to life.

But as I quickly learnt, there would be other seasonal hazards facing Australian city slickers like me and my Mum.

CHAPTER 5

A Hunting We Will Go

Princeton

Strange contraptions materialised in the Christmas tree fields. Steel ladders supported on mini-oil rigs disappeared among the branches of random oak trees. At their apex, timber planks were pressed into service as lookout benches, although in one case, a leather-upholstered base and back, resembling a stage-coach driver's seat, replaced the hard planks. I immediately pulled at my leash to clamber up on them. From these precarious platforms, red cardinals or blue jays might be watched. Traffic routes of deer and wild turkeys could be monitored incognito. Sadly, however, bird or wildlife watching was not the intention. Deer hunting season had arrived, a sport that partly provides the justification for the gluttonous stockpiling of guns that Americans pack away.

Dad permitted Fred and another friend to hunt on his land as long as they only used bows and arrows, rather than rifles. An unwritten agreement prohibited hunting when he was working in the fields, and when Mum and I took our walks.

To prevent being mistaken for a deer, people – and even dogs – painted themselves near fluorescent with 'blaze orange' or 'hunter orange' apparel. While the colours looked positively sickly on most, everyone drilled into everyone else the necessity of wearing them.

Just put 'mistaken for deer' into Google and many accidental shootings appear. On 1 January 2012, a woman in Norton was shot by a hunter, while on 9 December 2014, the Boston Channel reported a man shot in Hyannis while jogging with his dog.

One of the most long remembered tragedies was the death of Karen Wood over twenty-five years ago. She 'may have been hanging laundry...or...trying to warn hunters that they were too close to houses', the *Bangor Daily News* recounted in November 2013. 'And she was wearing mittens with white palms, which...may have been mistaken for the tail or "flag" of a fleeing deer...And the saddest part of all: Some local Mainers...blamed Karen Wood...saying the mother of young twins should have "known better" than to be close to the woods while not wearing orange clothing during deer season.'

No question, adjustments were going to be necessary by those of us from down under. As nearby gunshots mounted, Mum bought me an orange harness to match my leash and collar. And when the cool wet descended as autumn deepened, she threw a high-visibility orange rain jacket with toasty wool lining over my fur for good measure.

Fortuitously, Princeton University's colours are orange and black. As an alum, Dad supported any activities or attire related to his alma mater, so Mum's protective gear was easy to come by. An orange Princeton rain jacket and Dad's orange woollen Princeton cap became her cold weather uniform.

Hunters also wore orange; it wasn't just for the hapless.

Why, you might ask? Simply put, deer apparently cannot detect this colour.

Even with our orange outfits, we moved on high alert. I would freeze – muscles taut and head cocked – as gunshots echoed across nearby fields on weekends or weekdays, mornings or afternoons. This went on for weeks on end, and Princeton garb was not security. A stray bullet or over-enthusiastic hunter might infiltrate our property. Mum's additional precaution of yelling, 'Person and dog walking, person and dog walking – don't shoot!' didn't seem to help.

At the sound of these shots, geese feeding or resting nearby during their migration south took to the skies. They squawked and circled in majestic V-formations before deeming themselves either safe to return to ground, or better off resuming their journey.

Deer remained prolific, undeterred. They trampled vegetation, ate crops and rubbed against the Christmas trees, ruining their lower boughs. And since I came from a distinguished lineage of hunters back in England, my hunting instinct was on daily demonstration as I went about my forays in the fields. I barked at any deer I heard munching on the lush grass surrounding the barn. Mum, too, alerted them to our impending arrival, calling out, 'Time to move on,' particularly when she spotted the dappled twin fawns that frolicked around our house.

I would sigh. Not since 'capturing' a decidedly dead bird and proudly taking it into Mum and Dad in Sydney have I managed to come even close to demonstrating any meaningful hunting skills. Regardless, I made figure eights in the fields, nose to the ground, tracking scents left in their hasty escape.

I scanned under the Christmas trees for hints of movement. But other than chasing the deer from our property, my skills were clearly in the smelling rather than the catching line.

A whole industry existed around the army-style accoutrements hunters wore, decked out as if protecting America from imminent forest invasion. But it was the gun industry and its supporters that were so at odds with what we in Australia accept as normal. Following one massacre in Tasmania twenty-five years ago, a Conservative politician introduced stringent rules without any substantial pushback. Mum and I grew up with checks and limitations on the arms Aussies could own.

In America the opposite prevailed. The gun lobby was formidable and influential, successfully pressuring many lawmakers to preserve the status quo. Even in the face of frighteningly regular school shootings – the most haunting and scarring being the Columbine High School massacre in Colorado in April 1999, the Virginia Tech shooting in April 2007, and the Sandy Hook Elementary School carnage in Newtown, Connecticut, in December 2012, not long after we arrived – only token and ineffective changes have occurred.

While Mum waited for our car to be serviced at the local Jeep establishment, a cowboy straight out of Hollywood walked in, his gun proudly displayed in a leather holster on his belt. 'Who did he expect might attack him when he was having his car serviced in Princeton?' exploded Mum to Dad on her return. Something appears to be amiss, at least to ordinary Australians.

Mum became adept at quoting statistics at rapid-fire speed.

'There are more guns than people in the States. An

independent Geneva-based research project, the Small Arms Survey, related that in 2018, US civilians had 393 million arms, 46 per cent of the worldwide total, with 120.5 firearms for every hundred residents.'

But these statistics failed to impress. Sad were her contemplations of the country in which we lived as the months turned.

'This beautiful and free land has taken the definition of liberty to inexplicable, unfortunate and tragically, too often, fatal extremes,' she said.

How Dad's ears pounded, other people turning quickly away. At least I could absent myself for a snooze or squirrel rollcall when the umpteenth iteration commenced.

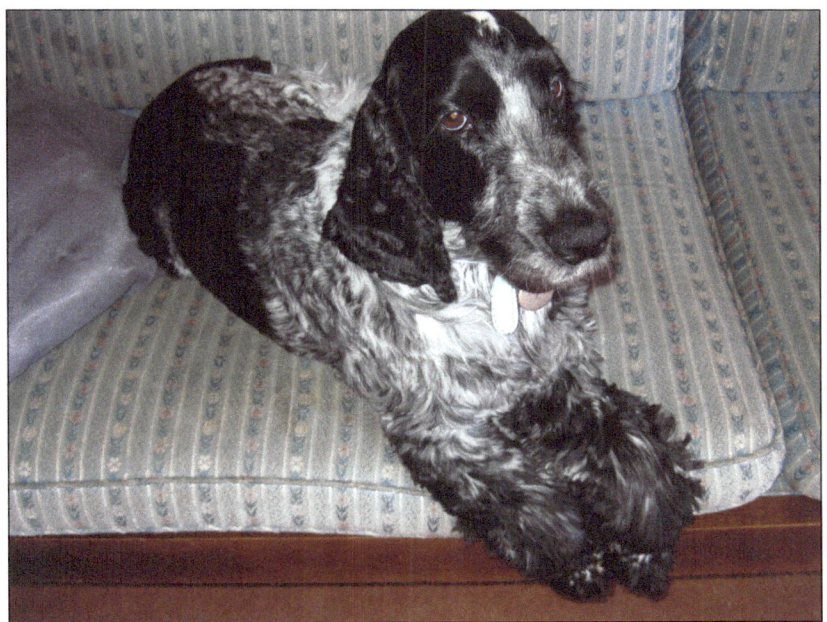

Here I am as a young man in Sydney before I left on my big adventure to meet Uncle Sam.

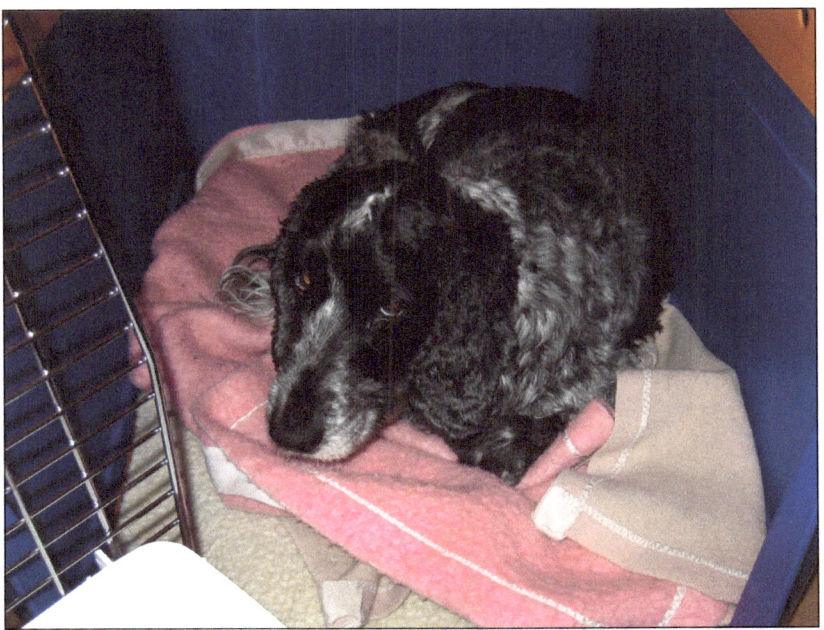

The dreaded mini-RV for my long-haul journey to and from the States.

I loved to get up close and personal with my Aunty Abby.

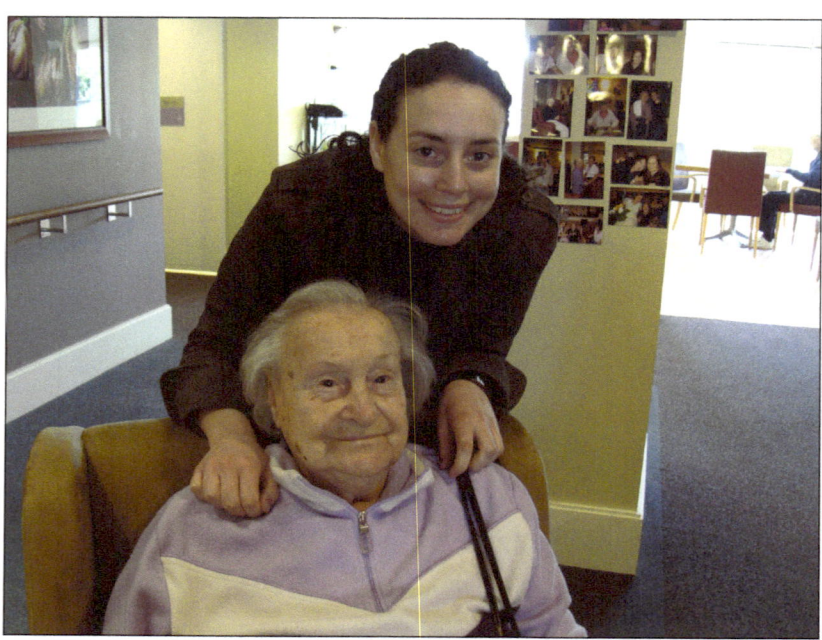

Sapta and Aunty Abby.

As Halloween arrived so did my first harness, which I was happy to model.

It was 'mums' time with beautiful yellow and white pots for me to manoeuver around.

Observing the squirrels and groundhogs from my prison yard – as close as I could get.

Our Thanksgiving family celebration in Maryland with Shaun, Lucie, Dan and Alexandra (back row) and Dad, Mum and me (front row).

Lucie's famous Thanksgiving sweet potato mash with sugared pecans.

When it was too cold to guard my critters outside, I observed from a snug spot indoors.

Christmas in Sydney many years ago: Ilana, Mark, Frank, Abby, Chris and Heidy. Mum and I must have been taking the photo.

Comfortable in my sheepskin bed, in the sunlight under the dining table.

Aunty Ilana's famous one-off Christmas ham – none for me as pancreatitis would rage.

Nap time again – but this time on the lounge room couch and cushion.

CHAPTER 6
The Tick Magnet

Princeton, 2012
We had more 'tricks for young players' to learn in our new country – my arrival in the damp and mild fall coinciding with the biannual spell of ticks and their tickery. Before we knew it, my skin was as bumpy as the moguls down the face of Australia's Mount Perisher.

If you're unlucky, you might see a tick once in a dog's life in Australia. Where we lived in suburbia, they were virtually non-existent, flourishing instead in the warmer, wetter climes of bushland or swamps. As we didn't frequent these environs, I hadn't been plagued by them, though they eventually grew to be more prevalent in populated areas such as Sydney's eastern suburbs. Arriving in the States, we were total novices.

According to the US Centre for Disease Control and Prevention, four common tick varieties were found in our area – the American dog tick, the blacklegged tick commonly known as the 'deer tick', the brown dog tick and the lone star tick. These ticks fed on all sizes of mammals, as well as on rodents and birds, while deer and dogs were common hosts.

Thus, ticks fed on the animals that used our property as their road, roadhouse or home, such as mice, foxes, groundhogs and deer.

They also fed, clearly, on me.

Ticks will bite humans too, and can transmit pathogens to people such as Lyme disease, named after the American town where the debilitating illness was first diagnosed. As we discovered, it's not a big step for ticks to move from dogs to humans. This incited hysteria in our household.

Mum is a hypochondriac. So I was an outpatient at the local vet if I didn't eat my dinner with gusto or had a slight limp – even if it was only a bindi caught in my paw. While this neurosis ultimately would pay dividends, Dad said our vets could thank Mum for her generous contributions to their children's school fees. Why should Mum change this habit just because she changed country?

Within days of arriving in the States, we jumped on the treadmill of vet visits, the first appointment confirming I already had two ticks hopping around on me, with bumps evidence of their bites. Blissfully unaware of the dire nature of these settlers, I always enjoyed being the doctor's centre of attention, and impatiently awaited the goodies that reliably arrived from these surprisingly similarly uniformed souls. Twisted out of my fur with the tweezer manoeuver, my squatters were removed. Mum's eyes opened wide at her new unwelcome chore. Once the trespassers were evicted, I received my first Lyme disease shot and tick collar, designed to disincline the little buggers from taking up residence.

While the tick collar became a wardrobe feature, it took time to work and, in truth, wasn't completely effective for ages. Persistent lumps meant ticks needed to be excised. In quick time, however, this grooming grew unsavoury. Mum hid the tweezers behind her back and Dad grabbed the torch. I ran for cover, heart racing and mouth dry. But they formed a successful coalition and another tick splashed into the toilet.

Ticks also arrived home via Mum as we walked or via Dad, since he worked in the fields mowing the grass or pruning the trees. They seemed to drop out of thin air onto the table as Mum and Dad ate, or miraculously appeared on their skin, on or under their clothing, or nestled as a dark lump in their hair.

'I have to find a way to cover myself as completely as an Egyptian mummy,' Mum said, swiftly fed up with tick torture. A 'Dr Livingstone I presume' wide-brimmed slouch hat, or her orange woollen cap, covered a tight sweatband surrounding a small ponytail. Not one hair escaped into fresh air. For upper-wear, Dad's white shirt covered one of his white Ts, weather adjusted with a denim jacket or down parka, and topped off with the bright orange rain jacket in hunting season. Jeans alternated with knickerbockers, and regardless of the season, long ski socks ensured no skin was exposed. Finishing with steel-capped boots courtesy of one of Mum's previous working lives, sunglasses and gloves, no tick could penetrate that uniform without dying of exhaustion.

Mum employed the annual booster plus the collar as my optimal prevention strategies. I proudly paraded two necklaces – a white tick collar plus an orange collar jangling its Franklin township registration badge and my identification tag, the latter perhaps not so helpful since it still bore Mum's Australian mobile number.

CHAPTER 7
We Vet the Vets

Princeton, October 2012

As well as a slight neurotic and egocentric tendency, my pedigree breeding results in a less robust disposition than perhaps your regular mutt. In my case I develop pancreatitis if I eat fatty food. So, on Dad's exploratory expedition to the US to scout out any canine deal breakers, he knew he would have to solve the problem of procuring my diet food. Vets in the States, as in Australia, will not sell my food without a prescription. But with no animal yet in the country, a vicious cycle was about to ensue.

Thankfully our solution-oriented Brisbane vet provided written confirmation that I did indeed exist and did indeed require my 'scientific' food for gastrointestinal purposes. Proof in hand, a conveniently located vet agreed that Dad could pre-purchase my food.

That relationship in place, it made sense for this establishment to be the first port of call when I required a consultation. With my sensitive tummy, habitual ear infections, lifelong dry eye, and instant attractiveness to the local ticks – and given Mum's predisposition – a visit occurred post-haste.

The attending nurse did the preparatory work, noting my details and history, heaving me onto the examination table and holding me until the hallowed vet arrived. This gentleman recommended the aforementioned Lyme disease injection and preventative collar. With our confidence built, we returned regularly over the next few weeks to have a tick or two removed, or to check my ears, which had already begun to itch.

We consulted two doctors at this practice. However, both irritated Mum when neither could lift me onto the examination table, a task reserved for the nurse. Two further issues sounded the death knell for this practice. First, Mum admitted she was paranoid about ticks but the second vet we consulted stressed that he wasn't worried about them. He then proceeded to suggest a treatment opposite to that of his colleague.

The final straw was when this tone-deaf vet advocated a course of allergy vaccines. I'd had this treatment in Brisbane where the subtropical vegetation caused scratchy and gluggy ears. Requiring a shot every three weeks, it was onerous even for a sickness-averse hypochondriac, so Mum closed her mind to rekindling this regime, justifying this view – 'due to the different climate in the States' – though even I questioned this logic.

Contrary to most dogs, I enjoyed vet visits. Early on, I sniffed out the treat tin and barked until I was rewarded. Without fail, vets did it my way. Treats were dispensed on the basis of increasing proportionality to noise and time. Therefore, I liked this practice. Goodies were generously doled out and the shiny waiting room was spacious and rarely busy. Thus, I was usually everyone's focus, another of my key vet selection criteria.

Unfortunately, my opinion was not sought, and we were off searching anew.

Closer to home, the next vet was like a lady in a 'Little House on the Prairie'. Reminding Mum of the empathetic female vets I'd had in Brisbane and Sydney, she also paid attention to Mum's dissertation about my medical history. With a profusion of treats on tap and bonus points as pieces of cheese appeared out of her lab coat top pocket – pancreatitis be damned – I gave this practice the paws up.

Practice number two went well for a while. Mum took Dad to see if he also approved. Recognising the micro-match to our Australian vets, he initially agreed. However as both became concerned there was no second-in-command on hand, they researched a contingency plan.

Soliciting neighbourhood recommendations (better late than never), Mum was constantly directed to one large practice. Further from home but with many vets, the doctor named most often received an investigatory booking. Able to lift me onto the examination table himself, plus treating us as if we were his only patients, this gentleman skyrocketed to favour.

As the vet trial and error route ground on, itchy ears became menace number one. With the onset of allergy season, aggravated by misplaced visits to the adjoining newly cut wheat field, a scratching frenzy ensued. My rear legs pedalled and scratched my ears and tummy, feverishly interspersed with much licking of paws and privates.

After a few nights' disturbed sleep, we headed to practice

number three – selected for that visit through a totally unclear decision-making process. Our vet mulled treatments of tablets, lotions or shots – happily settling on a successful tablet solution. This practice, however, was very popular. With many vets on duty, the waiting room was full, particularly on the occasions appointments weren't necessary, when we often had to wait up to an hour.

Taking after Mum, patience is not my best attribute. I barked with exasperation when someone was called ahead of me until Mum plonked me onto the bench next to her. Everyone else and their charges eased away. But once, a large white poodle called Polly shuffled forward to flirt with me. Against my barking, Mum tried to chat up the granny supervising her visit.

Polly sidled up and introduced herself, but then had the audacity to ask, 'What on earth is that strange accent you have?'

'I can make the same remark about yours,' I said. 'Mine comes from a very privileged heritage of English ancestry and an Australian nationality.'

Polly regained my interest, however, when she admitted, 'I don't know my background. I am a rescue dog, like many here in America. We're lucky when we become pets of wonderful families. In my case I'm also a precious grand-dog, so I get doubly spoilt.'

While I would have liked to question Polly about the meaning of the terms 'rescue dog' and 'grand-dog', she was summoned for her consultation.

Mum's vet choices brought my health under control and boosted her reputation as the go-to voice for advice on vet practices – or, come to think of it, on any topic she felt warranted her comment.

On the cusp of a holiday to Asheville with Dad, she wanted to be sure I was ship-shape before I vacationed at my dogsitter Jeff's sunny home in Warren, New Jersey. Jeff's personal attention in his ground-floor haven, complete with plush carpet and velour lounges, meant a pleasant respite. But having found two bumps, Mum wanted to check they were the finale to bites from ticks she had already purged.

Waiting at our closest vet's, a short-haired, short-legged brown dog in an upside-down ice-cream cone sat quietly opposite us with her stylish and petite French mum. Both mums took an immediate liking to each other. Chatting with the apparently recent arrivals, Mum proffered advice about the local gyms, cafés and walking trails – activities that fill the day of new immigrants such as herself.

The dog glanced shyly at me but was quickly taken to have its stitches removed. I shifted into barking mode to ensure everyone was primed. The cheese arrived promptly while Mum and Elisabeth arranged a walk in the woods.

Subsequently, Maya and her brother Boston, a white-haired anti-social terrier, became two of our regular walking companions. As comfortable ignoring them as they were ignoring me, I could get on with sniffing trees and bushes without distraction – a sign of true friends who understood each other's preferences.

A towpath along the Delaware-Raritan Canal was a regular route Mum and I walked with her other new friend Victoria and one of her two large black-and-white hounds, Kate or Hannah. Victoria couldn't bring both girls for a walk at once as they were strong, tall and, at around 20 kilos, too much for their slight mother to manage – particularly if a deer or rabbit crossed their sights.

Unaware of towpaths from Australia, Mum scoured Dad's bookshelf-laden walls, unearthing L. J. Barth's history of *The Delaware and Raritan Canal at Work,* published in 2004. We learnt a towpath canal 'is a man-made waterway that carries vessels from the interior to the coast'. The towpath adjacent to the canal is where mules or horses, 'harnessed together, walked…pulling the canalboats'.

Frequented by noisy walking groups, colourful cyclists, the odd horse rider and miraculously – finally – an abundance of dogs, the vegetation-lined towpaths provided concentrated smells of the wildlife, ducks and geese living there.

On Victoria and Mum's preferred walk, Lake Carnegie stretched majestically along the route, providing a liquid vista or, in winter, appearing as a frozen mirror. They hiked for almost two hours to the first bridge and back. If an aroma enticed Kate or Hannah and me, we crisscrossed our mothers and tangled our leashes. But if we both dived, I deferred, given the hounds' robust build.

Over time, the girls performed several disappearing acts. In one adventure, they escaped from the dog park where Victoria could take them both, ostensibly since they were in a contained area. Spying a hole in the fence, at a time of freezing temperatures, they followed a scent into the surrounding woods. Too fast for their mum to chase them, they became lost. Victoria made frantic calls to the local animal shelters and the police, and blanketed the area with flyers. Hannah wandered through the dense bush near busy

Route 1. A thoughtful driver saw her, stopped and took her to a vet, from which Animal Control united her with Victoria. Several snowy days later, Kate appeared on the deck of a house and was taken in by its inhabitants. Through the local animal shelter, where she was bathed back to beauty, she too was reunited with her mum. While shadows of their former selves, both were well, and wondered why their mum looked so worried, until they soon, thankfully, regained their strength and tone

Walking with Mum's friend Betsy and her white poodle, Parker, I ultimately learnt the meaning of the term 'grand-dog', when Parker's mum casually described her status as grandmother to her son's dog. Mum bragged of having two grand-dogs and a grand-horse back in the old country. A bond for both mothers, I was glad to be geographically removed and not share Mum with my four-legged relatives.

Parker and I became good friends, having been born three days apart and enjoying similar energy levels. Parker was overtly affectionate and indiscriminate in his licking. He was also indiscriminate in his attentions. If someone cycled past us, he would loudly voice his disdain – for reasons not apparent to any of us. Parker's mum called him 'squeaky Parker, the circus dog', with his talent for dancing on two legs while barking, or squeaking, at anyone resembling a postman.

Through introductions to Kate, Hannah and Parker, I learnt at last what 'rescue dogs' meant, as they were among that group themselves; their adoptive parents had rescued them from life in an animal shelter. Few traditions in America can boast such truly democratic principles. Common in the States for decades, I found out later that this means of becoming a dog parent became popular in Australia when Covid-19 hit. With families in lockdown for months, demand for dogs during periods of isolation outstripped supply. The rush to rescue a dog from an Australian shelter or pound was an upside of that terrible time.

With all my new mates, I had many changes of scenery. But like our mums, we also appreciated concluding our dates with morning tea or lunch, often at the Viennese café in Nassau Street. Under the umbrellas on the front verandah, we nibbled 'Greenies' or 'Schmackos', while the mums indulged in omelettes, Sacher torte or Blackforest cake.

Just like me, Parker eventually emigrated from the States, returning with his parents to Toronto, Canada, their original home. Similarly, Boston, Maya and their parents departed Princeton after two years for their home in Paris. Upon our return to Australia, pupdates ensued via the cloud, instilling connectiveness skills in us and our mums that would be useful in times to come.

CHAPTER 8

Thanksgiving

Princeton, Thanksgiving 2012
Thanksgiving was a highlight of our early days in the States. Dad's American stepdaughters, close but a study in contrasts – Lucie, olive-skinned with a former government career in Washington, and Alexandra, a tall, fair and slim artist – offered to prepare our first Thanksgiving meal and, just like Uber Eats, to bring it to us. With a stellar reputation for gourmet cooking and aware of our love of culinary feasts, Lucie and Alexandra vigorously embraced our eager anticipation, particularly following Superstorm Sandy.

Thanksgiving is an American national holiday devoted to celebrating the fall harvest and other blessings of the past year. Held on the fourth Thursday of November, families congregate and share a meal fit for royalty. For Mum and me, newcomers on the Thanksgiving scene, any holiday centred on a meal was made-to-measure for us. The Waldman reputation for food-centric single-mindedness was inherited by all Mum's children – Ilana, Abby and me!

In Dad's family, days of compiling ingredient lists and tag-teaming the aggressive shopping built to a zealous culmination in the early morning roasting of turkey and the all-hallowed stuffing. Rekindling memories of Friday night baked chicken dinners in Sydney or boiled chicken if I had an upset tummy, the aroma had me drooling over the kitchen floor, slippery saliva becoming a hazard of safety and aesthetics.

Lunch, stretching to dinner, commenced shortly after noon with nibbles of nuts, cheese and crackers, followed by the sit-down feast an hour later. The menu was so mouthwatering that anyone suggesting a change was roundly castigated.

Guests included the chefs, Lucie and Alexandra; Dad's lanky stepson, Dan, from Florida, and his mirror-image son Shaun; and Bettie and Fred from across the road with their California granddaughter, visiting from her eastern seaboard college. Jim, from the apartment below, and his sister from New York, plus Mum and Dad, rounded out the merry complement of eleven-plus-dog.

The huge turkey was the central attraction of the feast. Given the famous Griggstown poultry farm market was located just down the road, Dad offered to bake the turkey. A six-hour marathon to achieve the golden delight, this saved Lucie and Alexandra a logistical nightmare, while providing me with an elongated morning's supervisory job.

Ably carved by Dan, the turkey took pride of place on the table, which was laid with a 'stiff as a board' orange tablecloth, harvest-themed napkins, and two golden hued floral arrangements. Juicy and hearty stuffing, green beans with bacon – courtesy of Bettie – a refreshing garden salad, two platters of flaky warm buttered biscuits, and fluffy mashed potatoes formed impressive mountain peaks of smouldering tones. A gravy boater of Dad's famed orange and cranberry relish added a further dash of colour to the succulent feast.

The ultimate side dish was Lucie's legendary sweet potato mash with sugared pecans, a dish as sweet as any dessert, too delicious to stop at only one serving. The guests swooned. Lucie's recipe was in hot demand and thankfully included in her book *Dishing up Maryland,* so Mum could attempt a replication on our return to Australia.

Mouthwatering smells wafted between the open kitchen and the adjacent dining room, imbuing the house with an aroma akin to a cosy bistro. I zig-zagged between the guests as the platters were passed around the table, staring intently into each guest's eyes, in a perfect 'sit' position, wondering who would buckle first. Finally, perched at Mum's feet, I was rewarded with hand delivery of tasty morsels to my mouth, snapping me back to one Australian Christmas, nostalgia at its most spellbinding.

★ ★ ★ ★

Sydney, Christmas 2008
Rarely was Christmas celebrated as an extended Waldman family affair. However, in a year when the stars aligned, Chris' harvest in the States concluded in time to allow him to fly into Sydney on Christmas morning.

In addition to Mum, Ilana, Abby and Chris, guests included Mark, Ilana's yet-to-be husband, Mum's former husband, Frank, and his partner, Heidy. If former and future husbands being on the best of terms hints at the unusual, the event was also unequalled for the baked ham on the menu and the presence of a Christmas tree, both not the norm in our sort-of Jewish clan.

As the girls grew, a Christmas tree graced the entry lobby in Vaucluse on the sporadic occasions that Frank let his guard down. It reminded Mum of her childhood, when, living in a predominantly Christian neighbourhood, Sapta and Zeida adhered to local custom and a tree – of the lite-decoration and zero-light persuasion – sat on the landing near the bottom of the staircase.

Showing her age, Mum recounted one special homemade present, gifted from Mrs O'Flannery next door – a coat-hanger dressed in a little suit, its v-front open to store, of all quaint relics, *handkerchiefs* – complemented with a huge jar of milk chocolate-coated almonds. Mum's passion for the goodies never abated.

This Christmas, Ilana, Abby and I marvelled at the ever-increasing, brightly wrapped gifts giving purpose to the tree under the Vaucluse stairs. A spindly specimen from the local fruit shop and undoubtedly cut weeks before, this shrub cost three times what Chris would charge. Yet it still perfumed the air with a semi-pine scent that lent an air of credibility to the celebrations.

A brief shadow passed over Mum's face as we surrounded our scantily decorated tree, a few strings of glitter and a dozen red balls the sum token of the Waldman family's Christmas possessions. As her gaze alighted on me, flanked by her girls, her eyes moistened. Alone of all gathered, I understood the turn of her memory. It flared for her Cockers past. First there was Blackie, her guardian as a toddler, who exhibited his hunting instincts in the urge to chase cars – which ultimately cost him his life. Next, was her best friend Rexie, collected on a dry and dusty summer's day from a barren suburban backyard, when he ventured forward from his litter and picked Mum. She never forgave herself for abandoning him – her grief-filled belief – when the family moved home and he remained at her childhood residence, till she filled the deep well with my predecessor Bobbie. And then, for good measure, with me.

I sidled up to Mum to break her trance. Smells wafted impatiently from the kitchen. Formalities of present giving and suitable exclamations were speedily dispensed, thankfully considered by all to be the secondary precursors to assembly around the large kitchen table to eat the unusual repast – a change not only from the usual cold seafood, but also from the normal chef and guest roles.

Mum herself baked the small turkey that wrestled the little tree for scent supremacy – winning hands-down in my view and being the only time in my life that such a bird graced our Australian dining table. Ilana outdid herself by making a leg of ham, the diamond pattern scored professionally on its crunchy crackling. Served with a large green salad as the healthy option, it was soon overtaken in the rush to devour the cheesecake, chocolate mud cake and the annual present from Heidy, a Christmas Panettone, a nod to why we were gathered in the first place – other than to gorge ourselves merrily in the spirit of the season.

Princeton, Thanksgiving 2012 and Annapolis, Thanksgiving 2013 and 2014
Snapping back to this different feast, I hunkered down under the table with a full turkey tummy and reminded myself, I

was also with family – just a different branch.

Our Thanksgiving meal commenced with thanks for the gift of family and friends, and concluded with the human guests wolfing down dessert, a succulent wedge of both sweet pumpkin and apple and blueberry pie. Available from the same market from which our turkey hailed, pies became our ongoing contribution to Thanksgiving feasts to come.

As everyone had appreciated my company in Princeton, naturally I was on the guest list for the return to the traditional Maryland location at Lucie's the following two years. And since America makes it easy for pets to stay in hotels, my parents and I had a choice of accommodation, settling on the Hampton Inn in Annapolis where all canine Thanksgiving holiday makers were welcome.

For each trip we followed a standard routine. We drove south in the morning with a stop for Mum and Dad's coffee and pastry – and my bowls of water and kibble – at the Starbucks in aptly named Middletown. Arriving at our hotel around noon, we took our luggage, consisting mainly of my food, toys and bed to our room, changed and headed to Lucie's house in an upmarket suburb past the Naval Academy. Given winter was almost upon us, plus in honour of the formality of the occasion, Dad reverted from jeans to his 'uniform' of navy blue slacks and white shirt. Mum wore a black woollen skirt and knee-high boots for the only time during the year. Still, I stole the show in my red tartan wool-lined jacket.

We pulled into Lucie's driveway in front of her 'neat as a pin' home. Completing the second row of car pairs, we left the quiet streets of the neighbourhood vehicle-free, mirroring a pattern adopted outside every one of the freestanding dwellings in the tidy precinct. The suburb was a surreally people and pet-free zone, other family gatherings apparently either underway or to kick-off at a later hour.

Inside Lucie's place, the other guests were already gathered, including Dan and Alexandra, Shaun and his soon to be wife, Lauren, Lucie's stepsons, and Lucie's creative writing buddy and her son. Excluded, due to my arrival, was the gentle and little white rescue Lulu, Shaun and Lauren's dog, with Lucie's Siamese cats relegated to her bedroom. Oblivious to these modifications, in I bounded. My nose guided me to the turkey 'resting' before being carved. My sentry duty swiftly curtailed, I was escorted away. Eventually seated between Mum and Dad at the furthest end of the oval-shaped dining table, they tried to make my presence unobtrusive, a challenge as I launched at their plates.

While I thought our table setting had been elegant, it couldn't compete with the white starched tablecloth, bone white china, silver cutlery, crystal glassware, and the intricate fall floral centerpiece Alexandra created from plants in Lucie's garden. Set in a gracious dining room adjoining a luxurious lounge, both rooms held magnificent antique chests, passed down from Lucie's grandmother.

Intermission depended on the weather. If mild, we strolled as a loose group, admiring the picture-perfect homes set in manicured gardens now full of waving neighbours, squealing children and barking dogs. Another option, regardless of temperature, involved playing a raucous guessing game in small teams. The objective of the quiz was to answer ridiculous numerical questions as close to, while remaining below, the correct number. For example, one question asked the length of the Statue of Liberty's right arm. With much squealing and cackling, jolting me from my post-prandial nap, Mum and Dad once won the first round. I'm sure they had no strategy – rather a hearty dose of beginner's luck.

The compulsory finale each year was the family Thanksgiving photo posed at the fireplace, ably taken by Lucie's stepson, a professional photographer. Of course, yours truly, a valued family member, was included. By early evening, tired from the intellectual efforts and from posing for the camera, as well as from constant attempts to prevent me from discovering the leftovers – or the cats – we headed back to our hotel. After a disturbed night marching up and down the fire exit stairs and around the lawn for my comfort stops, we drove north to Princeton.

The day following Thanksgiving – Black Friday – officially started the Christmas tree harvest. Our day, then, developed far differently from the norm. Famous for its mammoth one-day sales, Black Friday was usually a vacation day. Mall carparks overflowed and impatient cars snaked in long lines along the main roads.

For us, Black Friday transformed our fields into gun-less hunting grounds, customers eager to get their tree while choices abounded. Dad turned into our driveway, flipped into Santa salesman mode, and greeted the eager, scattered crowd.

Part Five
Winter

CHAPTER 9

The 'Choose and Cut' Experience

Princeton, December 2012–2014

Harvested several days and sometimes weeks before sale, wilting Christmas trees in Australia's summer would be propped against the florist or greengrocers' windows to be carted home unceremoniously in the boot or back seat of the car. A number ended up being delivered with the fruit and veggies, their sappy boughs as flaccid and dehydrated as wilted sticks of celery.

In the States, 'Choose and Cut' Christmas tree farms like Dad's threw open their gates for the harvest, and offered, as our website proudly declared, a 'memorable family experience'. But these three words belied the painstaking preparation Dad personally undertook.

Prior to the harvest, Dad mowed and re-mowed the Christmas tree fields to golf-course perfection. He manoeuvered alternate Graveley tractors – one often being sent to 'hospital' just at a critical juncture – along and between the rows of trees for hours every morning. Tempting scents exploded with each pass of his mower, but bore fruitless results, no doubt the wildlife warned off by the mower's belching smells and guttural sounds.

Dad often bobbed up behind a tree, over a crest or at the edge of the plantation as we strolled by. He and Mum would enjoy a quick chat before we resumed our walk. When his efforts meant we could have played lawn bowls between the trees, his final chore was to remove creeping vines knotted into some of the trees and broken branches littering paths.

Then the winter wonderland was ready.

For the next four weeks, Dad's priorities were to greet his customers and sell trees. In an Aussie slouch hat, shredded red plaid shirt, faded and torn blue jeans and Princeton orange parka when it snowed, he was the community curiosity. A joyous mixture of Santa tummy and Pa Kettle outfit, he was Master of Ceremonies for new and returning customers, for one and for all.

Dad oversaw every activity. Before Thanksgiving, he piled placards into the car. With a 'howdy' to neighbours at strategic sign-posting locations, in exchange for a free tree, he sought permission to post a notice on their property directing passing cars to our harvest. A routinely successful courtesy, he then completed the cold, lonely and back-breaking job of hammering signs into partly frozen ground. This marketing accounted for almost a quarter of his sales, another half from word of mouth and return customers, with the balance from the internet.

As Dad's presence on the internet grew, his market changed. In the old days, so he told me, he knew everyone who visited – partly to get their value-for-money tree, but also partly to see their old friend, the *patron*, and share a chinwag. Dad thrived on these reunions and lamented purely transaction-based sales – tyre-kickers, he called them, out to get a deal, who could barely muster a 'Good morning'.

Overjoyed to see the influx of cars on Black Friday, Dad was like an alcoholic with his wine. The arriving crowds infused him with energy. Wherever I turned – he was there. Though no longer able to do any heavy lifting, he doled out gloves, kneeling boards, saws and twine, directing customers with advice and taking payment.

As soon as Dad's helpers arrived, a junior and a senior high-school student (to ensure succession planning), 'set up' began. Dressed in layers of warm, waterproof clothing, they appeared punctually at 9am and stayed till dark. Industrious, they agreeably undertook any tasks, while lathering me with pats to ensure my friendship. In our first year, the junior won Mum's heart by finding a couple of ticks on me and removing them. He also willingly scaled the stepladder to place a glass angel on the high leader of our Christmas tree. Another year, a senior from the local high school inculcated his friend into the junior role. She followed him to become the next year's senior. With remarkable technical, sales and leadership skills, she became baler assembler and senior operator as well as Dad's trustworthy and astute deputy.

Perched indoors at the large picture windows, I supervised the students zipping back and forth. They tied yellow 'caution' tape to poles to define the car park and paths, laid black duckboards to protect the grass from becoming muddy slush, and replaced the baler's netting. On weekends they lugged saws and kneeling boards to wheelbarrows at the sales hub, the belching metal barrel and chimney adapted into a fireplace, returning it all to the shed at day's end.

From their elevated lookout across the creek from the carpark, Dad and the students welcomed customers with the introductory spiel about safety and cost. They directed customers to the Blue Spruce or Concolour Fir fields, depending on family preference. Knowledge about the choice of tree was critical so customers understood the attributes of each species. The students – and I – learnt Dad's patter quickly.

'We have two types of trees. The traditionally shaped Blue Spruce trees are wide, dense and lush. Their needles are prickly, so wear gloves when cutting them, but their strong branches mean they can carry heavy ornaments.' Meanwhile the Concolour Fir, a niche selection favoured by a more limited customer base, 'are fine trees and emit a fragrant citrus scent when cut. Their soft needles, however, make them attractive to deer as scratching poles and thus the lower branches can be damaged. Comfortable to touch and easy to decorate, they require lighter ornaments that don't cause their branches to droop.'

The 'Choose and Cut' experience was joyous on mild, sunny days. Young and old couples, families with bouncy, shrieking children and eclectic groups of friends streamed from cars to the fields and back, hauling a procession of trees. Often doubling as a picnic, adults lounged under the walnut trees as their kids exhausted themselves with ball games.

Dogs, too, accompanied their owners, creating a parade of breeds unrivalled by any of my State-side experiences. Tiny brown Chiuhuahuas, mid-size grey Poodles, large cream Labradors, huge Saint Bernards and Rottweilers bounded out of their cars, many sporting wardrobes that could have appeared in *Vogue*. Catching a whiff of my existence, they sniffed around outside my yard, marking my fence posts in a typical fashion. Mum explained that we briefly had to share, but I worried when wildlife smells were subsumed. An early morning walk – thankfully – confirmed that deer and foxes only briefly disappeared, retaking their traversing rights after dark.

When rain bucketed down, a gale blew or blizzards hit, sales paused. The students joined me by the fire and did their homework. When the billiard table beckoned, snooker outbid their studies. Fortunately for Dad's sanity, these breaks were short lived, as most customers' urges to get their trees generally had them disregarding forces of nature.

Much to my chagrin, Mum's attentions were distracted from our normal walking, lounging and lunching routine by the two jobs she held during this period. One job was to feed our workers their pre-work cookies and hot chocolate, their fast-food pizza or lasagna lunch – always satisfying favourites, and often surreptitiously shared with yours truly – and their afternoon tea of almond nougat or gingerbread. The kids topped-up Mum's hot chocolate by boiling water, complete with marshmallows, on the outside barrel fireplace.

Her other role was to choose and decorate our tree. Dad, the students and I trailed after her around the fields like a poorly disciplined army on the first Sunday of the harvest, as she hemmed and hawed between different sizes, shapes and heights. Her Blue Spruce choices grew taller and fatter each year, starting at around 3 metres and climbing to 4 metres the following year. Dragging the majestic specimens into the house and standing them in ever sturdier tree stands again fell to the students – under Mum's and my command. Eventually she became enamoured with Concolour Fir, loving their orange scent and no longer having to wear gloves to dress the tree.

Decorations increased over time. In our first year we were light-free, Mum never having had lights in Australia and not realising their 'WOW' factor. By the second year we had a few strands, but by our third year our tree glowed, laced with rows of acorn-shaped and diamond twinkling lights. Turned on at dusk, they provided a sparkling vision for customers and a marketing tool for Dad. After laying the lights, Mum laced the trunk with thick gold glitter. A painstaking decision followed – which branch would each ornament adorn?

I grew increasingly bored over the four or five days of tree-dressing, during which my needs for attention and cuddles took second place. Whenever I wanted to play with one of the brown, red and green satin balls or silver mirror balls, I was castigated and informed they were not my toys. If one dropped and shattered – as they often did – I was quickly ushered out of the room. And on it went. Blue metallic deer, natural looking pinecones and green, mauve and light blue velvet balls brimming with beads, pearls and gems appeared from the endless supply of dusty cardboard boxes. As Mum moved up and down the stepladder, she gleefully unearthed ornaments with the most special of memories.

The 'Downton Abbey' red ball replete with castle reminded Mum of the art tour she took, showcasing the program's extravagant costumes. For Mum, a new arrival in town, events like these provided a girls' day out and introduced her to a raft of social, cultural and dining experiences. Three-course lunches with wine and even an espresso, at Connecticut, New York State and New Jersey restaurants sounded like the highlight of the outings to Dad and me. A hand-painted ceramic scene from the Amalfi Coast recalled Mum and Dad's Italian holiday with Dad's Princeton class, a made-to-measure tour for Dad's seventy-something year-old colleagues. From Tuscany via Rome and onto Naples and Sorrento, they ate their way through traditional pasta, margarita pizza, Peccorino cheeses, zabaglione and gelato, to say nothing of drinking their way through the Sangiovese and Chiantis. Meanwhile a cone-shaped shell from Hawaii and a ball of shells from Annapolis contrasted with the Australian fauna such as koalas and kangaroos, and majestic horse collection, courtesy of Abby.

With time on my paws, I invented my own harvest role – Head of Security. I barked at the helpers, moving to an attention-seeking bark as we became friends. I barked at idle customers chatting in the parking area. And from the protection of my yard, I barked at dogs to reinforce their visitor-only privileges.

Sales patterns emerged. On weekends, morning sales were lighter, when shopping or church took precedence. By late morning, crowds picked up, peaking at dusk when last-minute customers eked out the waning rays of light before sawing became a safety hazard. During the week, customers were left to fend for themselves, most of them returning tree hunters who knew the ropes and preferred smaller crowds.

On weekends, a curious trend increased alongside inflating website hits. Customers lost all sense of proportion. They ignored Dad's introductory warning that 'seeing is believing'

– if their car looks too small to tote a tree, then it is! Their cars became trucks. Their small sedan was surely capable of transporting a tree 4 metres high on its roof. And since Dad's pitch was 'any tree, any height for the same $50 price', human nature dictated the desired tree was always the tallest. With disbelief, and at times anger, tales of a tree wobbling precariously on the roof for the one-hour return journey to New York – or worse – falling off on the New Jersey Turnpike, were not unknown.

But it's the 'Choose and Cut' experience that our customers craved. Nature instead of the internet cloaked their children's world. Adults remembered sights and smells of times past. Sawing in the crisp air replaced the gym. Children yelled 'Timber' and laughed with joy. What was really being sold here? If Dad's observations are a guide, the number of families increased during the Christmas 2016 season following the divisive presidential election. African Americans, Indians, Asians and Latinos came together with the historically far more prevalent Caucasians. Dad had only seen this diversity and sense of community once before – the Christmas following 9/11, which seemed to suggest that what customers were really purchasing was unity and sharing, whatever their heritage may be.

By the fourth weekend, the season wound down. Graveyards of stumps replaced scores of trees. Signs were dismantled, duckboards stacked and tape rewound. The vista through the fields opened and wildlife cautiously reappeared.

And still our Christmas tree sparkled – sending out its rays of hope for us alone.

CHAPTER 10
My Dietary Indiscretion

Princeton, December 2012

Eight weeks after our arrival, Mum embraced the American ritual of holding 'Open House'. This custom generally entailed inviting friends – with a dish of their own making – to visit, thereby saving the hosts much work and time.

In Australia this event was called 'Bring a Plate', and it was a form of entertaining that Mum had never mastered. She believed the hostess was wholly responsible for catering. She therefore declined every offer except for those of libation, which she knew Dad would welcome.

With Christmas approaching, it was a perfect opportunity to hold this 'Open House' party and cement our place in society. But since the date coincided with the first Saturday in December, Dad would be selling trees until dusk. A suitable arrival time for guests had to be negotiated. Mum wanted them to arrive before dark, but Dad would not be there to stand at her side. What to do? A start time around 4pm was agreed. Dad would almost be finished work, and allowing for stragglers, Mum could hold the fort in the meantime.

With twenty-five people expected, there was much to be

done. A grand Christmas tree was cut and decorated, the lounge room rearranged with seating in groups of three or four and Christmas music was selected from Dad's extensive CD collection. The glass dining table was laid with a bright red tablecloth to receive the platters of food – hopefully 'out of Sidnie's reach'. The round balcony table, indoors for winter, was set with themed paper plates and napkins to reflect our distinctive character. Signifying our Australian legacy, hard beverages to be offered were 'Yellow Tail' red or white, or beer. And judging by the number of glasses brought out of hiding, there would be more drinking than eating.

But with a Jewish heritage, where the quantity and quality of food takes primacy, Mum's attention was on the menu. In Australia, bite-size quiches were popular. Mum thought that in winter in America this hot snack made sense, a decision that finally concluded her long soliloquies on this topic. In Sydney, she ordered tasty smoked salmon, as well as mushroom, bacon (heritage set aside for these august occasions) and vegetable quiches from our local patisserie. Made fresh daily, they were perfect hand-sized portions, to be collected warm a couple of hours before the guests arrived.

In America, however, Mum had no idea where she could be equally confident of product quality. Having turned down all offers of assistance, she knew this as make-or-break. She settled on our local high-end supermarket where, as in all things American, a similar, but frozen variety could be purchased.

The culminating pressure on Mum, however, came from Bettie, of Hurricane Sandy and Thanksgiving fame, an esteemed member of the local Historical Society.

'Your party coincides with my Historical Society's "Greens and Goodies" sale just down the road at our church hall. You'll find yummy slices and freshly baked cakes, perfect for your guests, and all for a great cause!'

Mum felt the potent request and complied.

First thing the morning of our 'do', Mum duly arrived at the hall. Immediately a luxurious plate of chocolate cupcakes stirred her excitement, the dark tops decorated in red and green icing. Her pleasure multiplied at the sight of a dozen coconut-maple slices, oozing syrup all over the plate. Moist and delightfully homemade, they appeased Mum's guilt. Who would now care that every other food would be store bought?

Traditionally, early Saturdays in the harvest hadn't been ridiculously busy. However, this year, kicking off a trend, people streamed in continuously, meaning Mum had to do much of the preparation herself. She pottered around, crossing chores off her list. Radiant heat warmed the lounge room and the tree glistened in the sunlight. Fifteen packets of quiche waited in the freezer for eventual heating. Platters of sweets were pushed to the back of the kitchen counter. Diligently, I watched, poised for any opportunities to assist.

By mid-afternoon, Mum, pleased with her progress, put out nibbles and sweets. Corn chips went on the glass table to await dips when the guests arrived. The morning's purchases, covered with a napkin for insurance, were placed in the middle of the entry hall table. With me dressed and ready in my Santa Claus kerchief, Mum went upstairs to shower.

Sniffing around, my nose led me straight to the cakes. My heart thumped. I paced around the table wondering how I could circumvent Mum's precautions. Jumping on a chair eventually shifted it away from the table just enough to land one paw while the other balanced on the table. The plate was now deliciously within reach. And a napkin was no issue for someone of my intellect and focus – I would just eat it!

Saliva foamed and my nose moistened. I savoured the unusual scents and pounced. Along with the papers, I devoured four cupcakes and four coconut-maple slices before Mum returned with a heart-stopping scream, realising they were gone.

Did a carry-on ensue? While I felt none the worse, Mum freaked that my latent pancreatitis would not take kindly to the chocolate. Keeping her panic in check, she rang our multiple vet practices, finally gleaning an emergency number. A receptionist, more intrigued with Mum's accent than the unfolding crisis, suggested she call the American Poison Centre, who deemed I required immediate attention and notified an emergency hospital to expect me shortly.

With guests due to arrive in half an hour, the oven heating, and Dad in the fields, Jim, conveniently nearby in his downstairs apartment, was briefly considered as an ambulance – since Mum's driving skills had not graduated further than the immediate locality. But never having demonstrated any pooch prowess, his ability to assist was doubtful. Nothing was to be done but call Dad in from the fields. Mum would do double duty as sales manager and party host. I was bundled into the car as the first guests pulled up and my tummy bloated and gurgled most unpleasantly.

As I later heard repeatedly, Mum prattled on with a graphic explanation for each customer and guest explaining why neither Dad nor I could greet them. They were further educated about the procedure she imagined I would undergo – the pumping of the stomach.

'I don't really know what that is,' Mum said in distress, 'but it sounds very serious.'

With appropriate mutterings to confirm they were paying attention, her rendition intensified with each retelling. My absence disappointed the guests who had anticipated meeting the special dog who had travelled so far to their country.

After 45 minutes Dad and I arrived at the hospital and met Dr Barrie. She initially impressed me as your kind and gentle grandmother. She explained that her treatment depended on exactly what I'd eaten, so they discussed the ingredients in the slices and whether they might contain sultanas, apparently even more dangerous to dogs than chocolate. Fortunately, Dad had the foresight to take samples of the offending articles with him and so they both treated themselves in the name of science, forensically eliminating the sultana concerns.

My favourable view of Dr Barrie ended with her potions, which made me instantly regret the transient joy I'd had gulping down the goodies. But my discomfort was only going to worsen. Dr Barrie told Dad he could go while she completed her ministrations. Finally happy with my responses, she let me fall asleep, the pain departing with the light.

Back home, Mum aided the remaining customers while concurrently welcoming the guests until Dad returned about two hours later.

While the quiches were a great success, it was to be days before I would be interested in sampling one. Regrettably the remaining chocolate cakes and slices went uneaten, not going so well with wine and beer. The entire purchase, while benefitting the Historical Society and the hospital's bottom line, had not really helped anyone else.

Knowing Mum, this giant hiccup would have cast a pall over her socialising. While going through the motions of a generous and gregarious hostess, she would have been counting down the minutes till the last guest departed and she could instead count down the minutes till my return home.

Consequently, Mum and Dad were up at the crack of dawn the next day to collect me by the 7am opening time. Other than a new diet of multiple tablets and a shaved area on my leg from the hydrating drip, I was none the worse.

They, however, had two pages of instructions to follow for my recovery treatment over the next ten days. Admonished by Dr Barrie for allowing me to get near the cakes in the first place, they were strongly encouraged to 'ensure no dietary indiscretions in the future'.

And so it was that I missed my first 'Open House'. There's always next year, I thought, but Mum and Dad had learnt their lesson. For the next two years while their guest list grew, I was to be a 'most unfortunate decline'.

The following parties were successes in the eyes of the guests and the hosts. Mum learnt some new tricks – the food was catered and she engaged assistance in the kitchen. Mum's friendship circle and bonds also strengthened, and the merriment in general blossomed. And, while I hate to admit it, Mum relaxed since I was banished to overnight babysitting – with no chance of being near either festivities or feast.

Sadly, my red bandana lay discarded in the laundry cupboard, mourning its loss of a stage before an effusive crowd.

CHAPTER 11
Sidnie's Snowshoes

Princeton
The weather in the Southern Highlands of New South Wales can be bitter. When I entered the world on 3 June 2006, I spent my first weeks in the coldest environment I'd so far experienced. I remained indoors except for the rare mild days when Mum Rosie, Serena and my other litter siblings and I were taken out onto soft rugs to sunbake. Subsequent Sydney and Brisbane winters were tempered with wrap-around warmth, as our reverse-cycle air-conditioning exhaled its fraudulent breaths. I had never known there could be a freezing side to winter.

I couldn't say winter arrived with a bang my first year in the States. It began in late October with Superstorm Sandy and an early introduction to melting snow. Mild weather returned until another brief snowstorm in November. Tricked again, winter finally arrived with full-force in mid-December. Narrow, grey limbed skeletons dominated the skyline. Only our Christmas trees, their defiant evergreen fingers extended, provided dashes of colour against this wizened background.

With the first snowfall, my black, white and red tartan

coat that I would model at Thanksgiving appeared. Its soft, fluffy lambswool nestled against my back. I took to the snow with defiance, eager to preserve the robust reputation of my English heritage, so that when the inevitable questions came about how Sidnie had adapted to his first taste of snow, the answer would be – with gusto!

Mum wore her navy parka from skiing days thirty years before. The jacket only just zipped up as layers of thermals, skivvies and jumpers were enlisted to supplement its warmth. Since it only came to her waist, and even though historically fashionable, she now resembled 'The Michelin Man'.

'Thank heavens that old jacket no longer has to be beaten into submission,' Dad said when Mum returned from Australia with Ilana's hand-me-down – a longer, fitted Austrian black down parka, more in keeping with the times.

I finally experienced the snow Mum had foreshadowed. It glistened on the fields and feathered the Christmas trees' delicate branches. Suited to the temperature, I bounded into the crisp air and pranced across the snow. During the early winter falls, the snow kissed my nose and dusted up behind me, turning my black socks grey as we strode along, almost without getting wet. Following a fairyland blanketing, the air was so fresh it was hard to discern the scents of my forest friends. I clawed at the powder, searching for their hideouts until the ground resembled a pock-marked minefield.

This is a bit of alright, I thought, wondering what all the sackcloth and ashes had been about before we left Australia. Predictions of snow as deep as I am high – for days on end – were forecast with solemn nods by sages who had never personally experienced an American winter.

But then…around mid-winter, the texture of the snow changed to thick, wet sludge. Mum's feet, clad in rubber-treaded, calf-high aprés-ski boots, sunk heavily into the snow. Of a vintage matching that of her puffy parka, the boots had long leaked any waterproofing capability. In my case, the snow stuck to my tummy, tail and neck, but clung most tenaciously to my paws. It built, layer upon layer, so that I gradually gained unwieldy and sticky snowshoes.

I plodded along under the extra weight, the load increasing with each desperate step. Bowling balls of snow built all over my body. Walks curtailed, we returned home with a lot of pulling and even some carrying on Mum's behalf. Encountering the warm air inside, the snowballs dissolved all over the breakfast room, my bed and the lounge. I alternated between shaking, licking and eating the glue-like appendages to remove them from my fur. As the balls detached, they melted and a watery slide oozed over the floor.

A cycle did indeed build of grey, somber days and deep winter falls, followed by a snippet of the sun's meager warmth and the dirty mess of melting snow mixed with mud. We longed for the tundra-like white wonderland of early in the season.

Longed, that is, until early 2014, when we really learnt the meaning of a sustained, hard winter. At first we ventured out ambitiously, eager to cling to our routine, as days of snow built on an icy base. Mum plunged knee deep in the drifts. I sank up to my tummy in the thick sludge. Lifting each paw required a Herculean effort.

When the temperature plunged far below freezing, I skidded on sheer ice, descended into mounds of popsicles, or teetered in one spot while jagged, glass-like pieces bit into my paw pads. My head spun with vertigo as I tried to get a grip. The result of an unwanted ice-skating lesson or a feverish dog paddle in sticky ice cubes was that I refused to venture out until the drive was ploughed, and then only on the melted mix of snow and gravel that provided some traction.

Cars piled up on our road, sliding into the invisible ditches or skidding on black ice. A police car became a fixture inside our drive, ready for the next predictable accident as cars hurtled around the blind corner in front of the farmhouse.

I stretched out in front of the fireplace to await the spring thaw. I reconsidered (quietly) my initial disdain for those warnings and (perplexingly) my initial exuberance with this season.

CHAPTER 12
School's In

Hillsborough, New Jersey, 2013
Re-examination of my ardour for winter played out another way.

Routine has always been my security blanket. I loved my days at home – my walks interspersed with meals; my naps in spots at pace with the sun around the house. As fires crackled in Dad's study and the lounge room, I dozed when the spirit moved, my pink tongue peeking from my mouth. One ear remained alert to the fridge seal breaking or the click of the cupboard doors. Grunts of pleasure leaked unconsciously from my mouth. Life was good.

My wakeup call came one Monday morning after we'd had a few months to settle into life in the States. Mum felt guilty – the company of mostly invisible critters and the occasional play date wasn't adequate socialisation for me. Winter also meant that I often couldn't – or wouldn't – get out. I needed a change of scene.

Following an at-home interview to assess my fitness for attendance, and having somehow passed, my first day at Jane's school arrived. With tail between my legs and a knot in my stomach, I re-encountered the overpowering smell of my species gathered together at 'Day Care'. I readied to defend myself, memories of successful strategies at Mandy's in Brisbane flooding back. After several sessions there I had learnt to circumnavigate the yappy welcome party straddling her fence, blocking my every move. Ingratiating myself with Mandy, I snuck into the house and spent most of my enforced attendance asleep on her wide, soft bed. Now I'd have to exercise my brain again.

Pees on every clump of grass or shrub exposed through the snow, or on the fake red hydrant outside the entrance only worked for so long. Eventually Mum hung my leash, harness and jacket on the hook bearing my name, apparently just like the pegs for Ilana and Abby's backpacks at kindy. She shuffled me through the stable-like half door beyond which no parent shall pass. With me now in Mama Jane's custody, Mum bolted!

Appropriate for a 'super-size me' country, this American day care centre made Mandy's seem like a Lego replica. Jane's was huge in area, staff size, and numbers and types of dogs. At Mandy's, located in a medium-density residential area, she was only permitted up to six dogs at a time. At Jane's, I counted at least fifty, with about one staff member for every eight 'children'.

The 'Dog House' was a replica of a large doll's house and functioned as the home away from home for older, quieter, smaller or anti-social dogs like me. There were doona-like cushions to lie around on, and a huge deck for a constitutional when it wasn't knee deep in snow. A fully equipped playground with multi-sized balls and oddly shaped climbing apparatus earned it a five-star rating.

A separate building at the back of the property was called 'The Ruff House', designated for rowdier and larger varieties of dogs. Appropriately they had a vast, fenced romping area, a snow or sandpit depending on the season, exercise toys like huge pipes to run through and a mini-baseball field for the incessant ball games.

Although my companions were more subdued, I had to be initiated nonetheless into their turf. It didn't take long for the questions to begin. Following the introductory sniffs, I was asked, 'What is an English Cocker Spaniel like you doing in America, when we have our own American Cockers?'

This line of questioning was a new twist. While gathering my thoughts, a barrage of questions followed regarding my background and colours (a black-and-white Cocker seemed equally foreign). But other than the first somewhat aggressive question, the rest of the inmates were interested in learning about the new recruit speaking in a strange tongue. I decided answering honestly with a touch of grovelling was the best policy.

'I have come from a far-away land called Australia, where I had lots of brothers and sisters who are all show dogs. While I am only a pet, I am nevertheless having a charmed life experiencing this fascinating country.'

In response, a brown and white Beagle, a small white Poodle, a grey Schnauzer and a multicoloured mutt guffawed in unison at my accent. 'You have a very broad bark,' they announced, 'so you will have to speak a little slower if we are to understand you.'

Surrounded on all sides, I slowly repeated my country-of-origin credentials. But a white, wiry and clearly wily Fox

Terrier had picked up my earlier statement. He barged into the conversation. 'What do you mean you are only a pet? We are all happy to be pets, so are you saying you are superior to us?'

The other dogs nodded, yapped or barked in agreement, so I tactfully backpedalled. 'I am very happy to meet you all. It must be my accent that has led to this misunderstanding.'

With some fast thinking, I expanded on my obsequiousness. 'I'm sure you are all exceptional dogs.' I'd heard Mum say that, according to her American Studies course, 'exceptional' is often how Americans characterised their country.

Apparently this mollified them. On returning to school, on long-term half-day status, unless it was a snow or freezing ice day when I had a reprieve (just like American kids), I was no longer interesting enough to warrant an interrogation. I suspect the general consensus was that communication with Australians must have been lost in translation somewhere between the Southern and Northern hemispheres.

No longer challenged by my classmates, I observed the teachers and kept an eye on the treat tin. While I played the guilt card, acting like I'd been tortured when Mum returned, Mama Jane clearly loved dogs. A little frightened tyke spent the entire visit bundled into a papoose nestled against Jane's chest. Unfortunately, I was simply too big.

With my regular attendance established, Mum and Dad found an additional benefit – I was permitted to stay overnight. It worked particularly well if they were driving into New York for a show, Jane's centre being located on the way. One really had to be on alert for this sleep-over experience, but my time at Mandy's stood me in good stead. Jane slept in the 'Dog House' every night there were 'guests' in order to supervise her charges. In Jane's room her bed was surrounded with various size crates, left open, should this be an unusual sleeping arrangement for dogs like me. The prized position was clearly in the crate next to Jane's bed. Having proved my competence in Comfort Studies, I quickly sussed out this system. Therefore, the Saturday nights I was boarded, I never felt lonely or scared about being away from home.

The added benefit was that having been there on the weekend, my regular Monday arrangements were suspended. For another week I didn't have to count the hours till Mum returned, and I could get back to where I alone was top dog.

Part Six
Spring

CHAPTER 13
Flowers and Fur

Princeton from April 2013
Spring's rebirth began in late March. Tinkerbell waved her magic wand and awakened a rapturous cycle of flora and fauna, alien to me. A riot of colour illuminated, freshness invigorated, harmonies purred and, with trimmed tresses, I unfurled like the world outside.

Skeletal trees morphed into verdant mists. Pale buds and leaves brightened, and a delicious apple canopy enveloped the foliage bordering the Christmas tree fields. Green shoots and a tapestry of yellow, purple and blue flowers sprung up like rippling carpets.

Daffodils surrounded our pond and clustered randomly in the woods. These officially heralded winter's curtain call in April. Hugging the farmhouse, they spilled over our new green-fingered tenants' ceramic pots, Morgan and her family having departed for their own home. Known as the 'poet's flower', they took their scientific name after Narcissus, the mythological Grecian youth so captivated by his own beauty that he turned into the flower. They captivated, indeed.

Waves of other flowers followed the daffodils' burst. Lolly

pink, flash purple, snowy white, lipstick red and sunshine yellow explosions of buttercup anemones, irises, eastern redbuds and tulips dazzled, their sweet perfumes ensuring the air was thick with heavy fragrance. Pollen tickled my nose as I emerged from my walks sprinkled with fairy dust.

One Sunday we visited the town of Cranbury, perched on a bend in a meandering river. We walked the few blocks that encompassed the little town. Above us, crimson and cherry coats adorned entire trees, while at my level, flowers flooded garden beds like overflowing tubs of tutti-frutti gelato.

Pride in their grounds outstripped even the home-owners' attentiveness to holiday decorations. Primed for photo shoots worthy of *Home and Garden*, yards were manicured to such perfection that Mum said they could equal the magnificence of Sydney's Botanical Gardens.

Saturday mornings trilled to the sound of lawnmowers, the mastery of which was often outsourced to an immigrant labour force who sprung up as suddenly as Narcissus's blooms. Pulling bulky caravans of equipment, rendering our narrow road more hazardous than ever, these men materialised every couple of weeks to ensure the lawns were smooth as blankets.

For those with no lawn or garden? *No problemo!* Brimming terracotta or glazed pots of flowers to the rescue. No deck or balcony dared appear naked.

Our farm, surrounded on three sides by wooded national parks, had vegetation galore. Therefore Mum, with zero gardening prowess, wasn't disgraced. As long as our lawns exhibited the requisite diagonal pattern, we boasted a blend of natural and cultivated beauty.

Fresh air was heightened with scents of spring babies. I took to this birthing season with rabid joy in my leaps. Chasing wind through the fields one morning, I zeroed in on an unusual smell. My heart rate rose and my steps stilled. My nose twitched and my eyes narrowed. I wound and rewound my way through the trees near the creek and launched into a gallop. I knew I was getting close. At last, under a small Christmas tree, a little brown nose and small set of black eyes peered at me intently, trying to establish whether I was friend or foe. To the side, rustling through the brush, a brother or sister made its own decision and scampered into the nearby thicket.

Mum reined in my leash. What she called a baby groundhog took an exit path from its stunned spot to its underground home beneath the bushes and intertwined vines. I pulled frantically against my harness but the baby darted off.

The grey furry creature, the size of a large mouse, escaped into the same bolthole as its sibling. We gingerly approached until I detected the tunnel into which it had dived. Amazingly it hadn't scurried below ground but peeked out from a safe distance, its beady eyes staring straight at me. Perhaps its mum suddenly called, for it abruptly vanished. I keened for its return. Mum and I waited, too short a time in my view, but to no avail.

We continued our walk until I pulled Mum back. I was rewarded with another sighting of the babies, who had repeated their breakout and waddled back among the Christmas trees. I howled as my nose picked up their fresh scents and we played hide-and-seek among the trees. They dived under bushes where I was barred from following, re-emerged briefly, and took cover again before retreating into their protective burrow amidst the thick foliage.

Reluctantly we headed home. From my vantage point inside, overlooking the patch of lawn that tempted mother groundhog, I stared out and waited, hoping my new friends would also venture there. By early evening, first one and then both groundhog kids appeared to nibble on the grass.

I charged backwards and forwards, sliding wildly on the shiny floorboards between two long windows as I sought to improve my view. My crazed running, interspersed with barking and wailing, curtailed my outlook, however, as the panes clouded with my panting and splatters of saliva. But the clever babies must have already deduced they were protected by my glass caging. Ignoring my laments, they continued their meals. Eventually Mum and Dad could no longer stand my noise and worried that my shenanigans were probably disturbing Jim below. They walked out onto the adjoining deck, ensuring the fur balls spied the potentially more significant adversaries and took off in fright, returning when they judged the coast to be clear.

For weeks we continued our game of cat and mouse. First stop on our walk was the groundhog kids' playground where they always tended to wander. Mum was cautious that they were a safe distance from us, so I was only treated to the sight of them scooting away.

As cute as my groundhog babes, a particularly sweet brown-and-white-spotted fawn snuggled under a low hanging Christmas tree and stole the show. Left briefly by its mother while she foraged for food, its spindly legs not yet capable of walking, the baby lay stippled by sunlight as it awaited her return. Without a scent to broadcast its hiding place, we tiptoed away lest we inadvertently signalled its location to prey or scared off its mother as she returned.

Over spring my playmates grew fatter and wiser, rarely exposing themselves. I dragged Mum back to their original hidey-hole, even though there were only remnants of their scent. Ultimately, I had to accept the closing of the games.

My little mates had learned to hide out of my sight.

CHAPTER 14
The Goose Family's Travails

Princeton
Following their winter in Florida, like many American snowbirds, our pond hosted Mr and Mrs Canada Goose, a devoted couple who called it their spring home. Even though the pond bed was engorged with silt from upstream runoff, true to their instincts, the same pair returned annually to prepare for their family.

Twice daily, being as considerate for Mrs Goose as for our fawn, we trod quietly around the pond. From a distance we monitored the natural island where, under a pair of intertwined trees, Mrs Goose sat on her nest of dried reeds. Neck extended and head low, she peered at us.

Mr Goose was accustomed to our meanderings but diligently scrutinised the property for predators. He roamed the length and breadth of our land, ready to defend Mrs Goose as she protected her eggs.

With heavy hearts on successive days, we discovered one and then another, empty eggshell in the Christmas tree field. Dangers lurked everywhere – a snake or turtle from the pond, a crow in the air, the cunning red fox we occasionally glimpsed at the edge of the treeline. Any of these could have snatched the eggs when mother goose briefly left her post for a swim or a meal.

Yet she perched on her nest for weeks, occasionally preening herself and removing feathers to replenish its insulation, raising our hopes that several eggs remained.

With binoculars at the ready, Mum checked Mrs Goose several times a day, worrying whether she could shelter her eggs through the 28-to-30-day term to produce a family. To increase Mum's angst, Mr Goose often crossed busy Fir Tree Road to Bettie's property. Thankfully he navigated the dangers and returned to accompany Mrs Goose on her rare periods of respite.

The proud parents eventually rewarded us with a parade of three grey fluff balls. The goslings could fit in the palm of Mum's hand and almost disappeared in the spring grass. We remained at a distance, Mum watching through binoculars from inside for the next few days as they were exercised like a little army platoon. Their doting parents trooped them the extent of the property and taught them how to eat. Yet their insistence on marching the babies across the road for a change of grazing scenery posed a frightening and needless risk.

To manage the chilly nights, Mrs Goose enfolded them under her wings. However, since they couldn't fly – nor could their parents as they were moulting – the family took to safety in numbers, joining others near the canal. After losing sight of our Goose family for an agonising week, we finally glimpsed two pairs of parents shepherding their offspring between the Christmas trees. With at least eight goslings in tow, we were convinced three were our new babies.

Our peace of mind was short lived. The next day we stumbled across the body of one gosling in the fields, possibly caught by a fox and subsequently dropped when we approached. Mum was distraught at this cruel side of Mother Nature. Trying to appease her, Dad suggested that 'perhaps this behaviour is necessary so that Mr and Mrs Fox can feed their babies'.

Mum understood his message but was miserable.

Her despair wasn't over yet. A few days later, Mr and Mrs Goose reappeared with only one gosling in tow. The furry puff ball had doubled in size and scurried around with its parents, feeding voraciously.

The next day, however, we were woken at daybreak to honking as distraught Mr and Mrs Goose scurried around. This behaviour continued for the next two days, the parents combing the property and dipping into the pond as they looked for their last, lost gosling. The desperate blaring continued like a siren – and then nothing. We searched our property and across the road, but Mr and Mrs Goose, along with their baby, had vanished.

CHAPTER 15
Stags, Snakes and Snapping Turtles

Princeton
With the prospect of alluring trails and inviting scents, I barked greedily when my harness and leash appeared. The lush fields were now surrounded by dense foliage and twisted vines.

But ominous menaces waited.

Mum tried to warn me one still morning. I was nose-down scent-stalking, when, as we rounded a bend in our path, we came face to face with a huge, male deer called a stag. Usually invisible in the woods, the beast shot us a look, at once quizzical and untamed. Its throne of horns glued us to our spot. My heart pounded. I swore I could hear Mum's as she calculated we were no match in size or body armour.

His antlers spanned the width of his thick body. Three distinct branches spiked the air. Stags' antlers might be grown and shed each year, but during mating season, they were imperative for fighting one another for the attraction of a female. I sniffed the air to discern any presence of a doe. For once, I felt relief that there was not. Normally when a doe or a herd of deer detected us, either by sound or smell, we became an intriguing apparition. Then with a telepathic signal, one or all skittered away. Now we could be the ones who skittered off. Having decided we were no competition, the stag stood its ground, but let us go.

We pivoted and walked hurriedly in the opposite direction. Tail between my legs and head cowed, I feigned nonchalance, praying we weren't being followed. Mum didn't dare check until we were in sight of home.

The possibility of repeating this experience haunted us on future walks, Mum's eyes shifting around, her shoulders set for retreat or attack. Soon, however, she felt beset by all sides, and not simply from fear of a furious buck. The unusual amount of rain during the spring of 2013, one of the wettest on record, had resulted in triffid-like grass and weeds. No sooner did I detect an intriguing smell than Mum would pull me back. Tension wafted from her skin as I narrowly missed yet another slithering snake. The snake could have been an Eastern ribbon, garter or water snake, or any one of the roughly nineteen varieties that inhabit New Jersey. Their forms ranged from short, thin, brown to long, thick, reptilian grey or green-coated monsters.

Materialising near the pond or unexpectedly under a Christmas tree, the snakes raced away or froze if confronted. Yet the potentially fatal reputation of Australia's poisonous brown snakes bedevilled Mum and we scuttled away in a fright.

Our environment had more in store. Blundering towards a large rock, it abruptly moved. The dark grey shell camouflaged an ugly, forbidding snapping turtle. Mum knew they inhabited the pond, but she'd been unprepared for these freshwater turtles to meander widely through the fields to find burrows to lay tens of eggs at a time. After she breathlessly recounted this discovery to Dad, he explained that they covered large distances throughout the plantation.

The aged and unpleasant aroma characteristic of the snapping turtle taught me to be on guard. Mum watched me with one eye, while the other searched the soil for the tell-tale dirt trail. When confronted, the adults buried their faces under shells the size of two Marine helmets. Mum made sure I never drew close.

According to Wikipedia, a snapping turtle is 'noted for its belligerent disposition when out of the water, its powerful beak-like jaw and its highly mobile head and neck…Long-term mark-recapture data from Algonquin Park in Ontario, Canada suggests a maximum age of 100 years.' You can read more about these turtles here: en.wikipedia.org/wiki/Common_snapping_turtle

These surprises, and hazards, tempered Mum's enjoyment of the beauty of the countryside. To distract herself, she sang Leonard Cohen songs, her tone deafness acting as a natural threat deterrent. Slowly, as the weather became hotter, the menacing animals took to the shade of the thick forest, the damp soil, or the cool pond for relief. Our trepidation diminished, and it was a completely different angst with which I next had to contend.

CHAPTER 16

Mum Institutes Precautions

Princeton
When living in Australia, Dad's preferred routine had been to return to the States twice yearly to plant seedlings and then to mow and groom in preparation for the harvest. On his 'BS' visits ('Before Sidnie'), he would hire a car, since that made financial sense. With an expanded entourage, the time was right to buy one.

Travel on the country backroads was precarious at the best of times. The added risk of skidding on snow or ice lent weight to the purchase of an SUV. Elevated vision and four-wheel-drive capability were two benefits of succumbing to the trend. I had not been included in pre-purchase discussions. But as material seat covers would attract dirt or get wet and muddy with me onboard in rain or snow, Mum's preference for black leather seats was agreed to be most practical.

When the gleaming silver 4WD Jeep arrived with its new-car-leather smell, Dad summoned the courage to teach Mum to drive on the wrong (right) side of the road. At nearly 8 kilometres from our house to a major intersection, Fir Tree Road served as our regular practice corridor.

'Hug the centre, hug the centre,' became Dad's catchcry on our narrow and windy road.

Exacerbating the tension, Mum hit the brakes whenever a car or a bend appeared. To make matters worse, during early mornings or late afternoons, the sun's dappled rays played tricks with light and shade when it burst through the roadside vegetation. Dad was silent and stoic. I careened forward, almost hitting the rear of the front seat, or slid along the back seat as Mum strained to remember which side of the road to pick. These training sessions had a short shelf life. True enough, Mum and I increasingly drove alone. My status enhanced to co-pilot, I now rode shotgun, the wind in my ears, Snoopy style.

Early in Mum's autonomy, she muttered, 'Stay right, stay right,' shoulders hunched, steering wheel clenched, and pace measured. Remaining just under the speed limit, we were overtaken by endless cars regardless of double yellow lines and limited sight. Even as we approached, oncoming cars overtook cyclists in their way, relying on us to brake.

American drivers had other tricks in their repertoire too. Just as traffic lights changed in our favour, cars would turn directly across our pathway. As we approached, they would pull out from the curb or a side street directly in front of us. Business as usual also involved tailgating or texting while driving. Drivers were always in a hurry. Mum claimed that when an American driver gets behind the wheel, their psyche switches from sweet and gushy to aggressive and arrogant. Driving at least 15 mph over the speed limit seemed *de rigeur*.

She had to see if her experience was supported with facts. In 2016, WalletHub confirmed speed was a factor in 27 per cent of deaths resulting from vehicle crashes. Cars were regularly pulled over by the police. Data from the National Highway Traffic Safety Administration in 2014 showed that the average number of people who received a traffic ticket per day was 112,000, with 41 million tickets issued annually – over 20 per cent of drivers.

Speed also accounted for an excessive number of deer collisions. According to a national 2014 insurance report, West Virginia had the highest odds for hitting a deer, while New Jersey was rated as a medium risk. However, judging by the number of deer on the side of the road, legs splayed and guts exposed, deer may not agree.

★ ★ ★ ★

Monmouth Junction, New Jersey
Until Mum became familiar with our immediate area's services, my monthly grooming occurred at Pet Smart on Route 1, by an astute young woman called Sharon.

To reach the salon in the back of the shop, patrons had to navigate aisles of toys, clothing and food. A bewildering array of balls, ropes, furry animals and kongs adjoined collars, leashes, harnesses, coats and wet-weather gear in rainbow colours and reflective light and heavyweight materials. Treats ranged from mouth-watering chicken, liver and beef chews to rawhide bones with juicy fillings. The odours wafted our way as I tried to force a detour.

Following my bath and trim, when still enthralled with Sharon's labours, Mum trailed her to the harness aisle, all the while reciting her derisive spiel about American drivers. Sharon counselled Mum that New Jersey requires dogs to be harnessed in a car, deftly solving Mum's cultural and legal quandary. To conclude her case, Sharon added, 'If he's a pulling sort of guy when you go for your walks, a harness will take pressure off his neck and spread it more gently on his back.'

Always concerned for my health and wellbeing, Mum was convinced. She chose a black outer and sheepskin inner model and adjusted the straps to fit me 'like a glove'. Quite the fashion plate, I pranced proudly to the car. But instead of sashaying into the front seat as usual, I was popped into the back and the seatbelt threaded through my harness. While this arrangement allowed me to comfortably sit up or lie down, my co-pilot rights were thwarted. I couldn't even sit in the centre of the back seat to monitor what was happening up ahead. Nevertheless, this safeguard became the norm. Held securely in place, there was no more head banging or slip-sliding, and we could now pass New Jersey's 'click it or ticket' test.

The sorry conclusion to this story, however, was that after a few sessions with Sharon, she disappeared without explanation. Mum's tips, her sales commission and her quality time with me and her other clients had sadly not motivated her to stay.

Princeton
Although Mum's driving prowess improved to the point where we were rarely overtaken, her antagonism towards your typical American driver did not diminish. Instead, she identified other arguments to support her view.

She swore angrily when greeted at the shopping centre with supermarket trolleys spread about the parking lot like a measles rash.

The American love affair with convertibles was cause for even more contempt, particularly when the driver was of geriatric age. Roof retracted the minute it stopped snowing or raining, the convertible grilled the stupid people leathery brown, Mum would observe. What was it with Americans and their general disdain for a hat? she demanded – herself bred into good, common sense in the skin cancer capital of the world.

There were also frequent brushes with stony-faced drivers, cell phones in hand, speeding towards us, destinations alone on their minds. Other drivers lazily cut corners or asserted their right to the one-lane bridge.

In time, Mum found her preferred response. She gave the fingers-up gesture or would sit on the horn and swear. The first time this happened, I bolted upright from my nap, tummy tight, wondering how I hadn't noticed Mum graduate into an American driver.

Then there was her confrontation in the Princeton North car park. Alighting from her car, Mum spotted two dogs in a parked car. While not yet summer, it was sunny, and the windows in the car were not lowered enough to appease Mum's heatstroke concerns. In a rush to get to the dentist, she asked the shop assistant in a nearby framing shop to call the police and bring the plight of the dogs to their attention.

Returning an hour later, the situation was unchanged. As she would in Australia – Mum called the police. Stunned, the policewoman was not sure what Mum thought she should do, but finally concluded this deranged woman expected her to front the scene of the crime. While providing directions to the police, headlights on the guilty car flashed and the owner appeared, Mum berating her and educating the policewoman simultaneously.

'The police are on the phone and on their way here. They are about to arrive and charge you for leaving your pets in a hot car. If you were in Australia, your car windows would have been smashed!'

In American 'stuff-you' fashion, the woman blasted Mum and told her to mind her own business. The driver and dogs then promptly exited.

Recounting this tale over dinner with friends, Mum was reliably informed that, this being America, she could have been shot for meddling. She heard the warning – though her Aussie heart demanded that she still check parked cars for abandoned (if perhaps only briefly) pets.

And as Mum's confidence navigating our surrounds increased and we spent more time driving together, at least as far as the four-legged passenger was concerned, we thankfully became a family that took precautions.

Our Christmas tree glistened for all to see in its double-storey splendour.

Now that's a Christmas snowfall! On our beautiful border trees, just beyond my fence.

Santa and Snowman greeted passers-by along the canal.

Pa Kettle look-alike: Dad in front of our first Christmas tree in the States.

Guarding the presents pre-Christmas.

Our winter wonderland home in the converted barn.

The view from home towards the pond, raft-like bridge and creek, in the depths of winter.

Well, they managed to fit that tree into their truck's tray.

Spectacular spring flora in Cranbury, New Jersey.

Some of the joyous technicolour spring flowers along our walk in Cranbury.

Dad, between his sister-in-law, Wendy, and brother, Paul.

A statuesque white egret near our pond on the farm.

Cousin Dalia and I taking a walk along the canal towpath.

Mr and Mrs Canada Goose with their gosling.

Mum and Dad's day out in New Hope and Lambertville with their Aussie best friends, Max and Jane.

Dan after his mammoth cycling tour from Florida.

Relaxed sentry duty on the front deck.

My groundhog mate who lived under the shed and always stayed on his side of my fence.

Modelling my Princeton orange harness and leash as Aunty Ilana and I trod the canal towpath walk together.

Mum and Dad wearing Princeton University garb for the 55th reunion.

Dad's college roommate, Len, and his wife, Sue, joined us for the 55th reunion.

When the weather cooperated, a sunbake on the garden chaise beckoned.

Slumber alcove in Mum's study.

Another slumber spot – on the chaise in Mum and Dad's bedroom on my very own pillow and blankies.

Mum and me back home in Sydney.

A hearty warm smile to you all, from my home in Oz.

Part Seven
Summer

CHAPTER 17

The A and A B and B

Princeton from 2013

Hard on the heels of warmer weather, a conveyor belt of guests arrived on international pilgrimages from Australia or domestic visits from all points of the American compass. Our cedar home, perched majestically atop exposed stone foundations, was a welcome sight for many a weary traveller.

My job was to announce new arrivals with loud and insistent barking. This broadcast confirmed our own 'Homeland Security' was in place. Visitors knew who was running the show.

They would slide open the heavy glass doors from the deck and walk into the welcoming breakfast nook, relieved as air-conditioning hit them. The open kitchen floated beyond the entry like an island. Behind it and stretching the length of the house, the lounge, dining and billiard rooms appeared, beckoning everyone into the coolness. Hosts and guests gathered in the intimate, orange-toned sitting area, whether at the glass dining table with panoramic views of the pond and Christmas tree fields or around a full-size billiard table, eager for a game. First timers were amazed at the incursion of lush green from the myriad of double-storey windows and sliding doors. Sloping white ceilings, light cedar walls and polished blond floorboards offset dark brown beams and solid columns.

Dad's masculine book-lined office off the entry doubled as his hidey-hole – round-the-clock socialising never having been his style. Mum's sunshine yellow study halfway up the stairs, with its high sloping ceiling, featured a built-in sleeping nook and views peering deeply into the branches of the adjacent trees. I thus had multiple napping spots, to be chosen based on their prime deer-peeping potential.

At the top of the stairs, Mum and Dad's huge, light pale yellow bedroom held additional sleeping choices, ranging from the deep yellow velvet reclining couch, from which I observed every nocturnal turn, to my rust-coloured bed nestled against the armoire on Mum's side of their gigantic bed. Opposite their room, the generous, warm-white guest room was bright and toasty in winter, but tending to hot in summer, receiving sun from midday through the whole afternoon. Furnished with a new king-size bed, for which a small stepladder would not go astray, plus my day bed, the room sported light-blue floral bedcovers on both, matching the playful curtains. With separate ensuite and guest bathrooms, as well as a powder room – or restroom as they are known in the States – on the entry level, the house was well designed for everyone to have their privacy and desired amenities.

These features meant that guests were welcome as long as they were comfortable with me. A gentle hint to close the guest-room door tightly when bedding down for the night was usually enough to give them time out from the security guard.

Arrivals began in April, moving from a trickle to a flood by the warmth of May, June and July. A slight hiatus until September and October gave Mum and Dad time to enhance their food, beverage and tour-guide services. This annual pattern saw vacancies at the inn during the unbearably hot month of August and through much of winter, with only those prepared to risk a safe landing during the tricky snow and ice months game to come.

A special arrival was Mum's cousin Dalia in September 2013, from San Francisco. I knew Dalia well, having hosted her trips to Sydney and Brisbane. Mum's and Dalia's mothers were close, although they spent much of their adult lives in different countries. Dalia's mum remained in Israel, while Sapta and Zeida emigrated to Australia in 1948. But Mum and Dalia continued their special relationship, visiting each other across the world or now across the country.

Just around 160 centimetres tall, Dalia was a touch shorter than Mum but the same age and with similar brown curly hair. Born in Israel, she'd moved to the States as a young woman. Thus she spoke with a heavy Israeli-American accent and generally complained she couldn't understand Mum's broad Australian twang. With her being partly deaf to boot, it was amazing they could communicate at all.

Dalia's laugh was loud and warm, matching her happy face and adventurous spirit. An animal lover, she spoiled her cat Leila and ran a dog-minding business for small to medium dogs from home. Dalia was the first guest to grant me sleeping privileges. Free to sniff her luggage, I caught an enticing scent one night that wafted from the open suitcase where she'd flung a pair of black leather shoes. The soft leather and supple rubber soles reminded me of strengthening my teeth on Mum's new black patent leather Ferragamo shoes while she was away at work. As Leila's smell pervaded the leather, I gnawed on the shoes, giving maximum attention to the soles.

None the wiser the next day, Dalia wore the shoes to Lambertville, a town on the Delaware River full of art galleries, antique shops and a large choice of favoured restaurants, including a real-life 1950s milk-bar, with a counter, red vinyl stools and small, hard-backed booths.

Dalia crossed the road on her now unevenly balanced shoes. The gravel completed the annihilation of the rubber soles so that only the metal fixtures remained. Gradually it dawned on her that they'd provided a midnight snack for yours truly. Dalia was horrified – Mum relieved I hadn't cut myself. A good sport, by the time we returned from our outing, Dalia had forgiven me and appropriately chastised herself for leaving the bag open.

Our West Australian guests, who visited in summer 2014, introduced me to someone more my size. Unfortunately, their arrival coincided with the township's road-resurfacing program. With parking only available at Bettie's across the road, a gaggle of sweaty people appeared, dragging their luggage across our huge front lawn. In one of their strangely shaped rollies was a little sleeping person. When this small being awoke, she was not much taller than me. We studied each other and concluded we were both of a gentle persuasion. Henceforth we snuggled against each other on the orange lounge. While she watched 'Playschool' on her iPad, I dozed, a soft toy locked firmly in my mouth – just in case she mixed it up with one of hers.

A semi-regular visitor was Dad's stepson Dan, branded into my brain as the Thanksgiving turkey carver. We were his stop-over of choice, offering lodging, food and grog, on his cycling trip north from Jacksonville, Florida, to visit friends in New York State, where he'd grown up.

As a coffee aficionado, Mum drank an espresso twice a day – enough to keep her buzzing. Dan, however, was in a league of his own, brewing coffee first thing in the morning and downing several cups before – and in fact instead of – breakfast. While Mum watched with astonishment and admiration, his dearth of food was considered a sin by a Jewish mother.

Not so for Mum's best friends from Sydney, Max and Jane, who visited us a couple of times, Jane having been born in the States and with lots of cousins to catch up with. Early each morning, Max bounded into the kitchen. First he combined lemon juice and water, followed by apple cider vinegar and water – aids to digestion. An optometrist by profession, he then brewed a pot of white tea with saffron to prevent macular degeneration. Onto the solid portion of breakfast – a huge plate of pink grapefruit, blueberries, strawberries, kiwifruit, papaya and passionfruit, to be eaten with muesli and yoghurt. A cappuccino or two concluded the repast. We could only all watch with awe!

Particularly welcome, Mum's daughters Ilana and Abby also brought a bit of the old country with them. Although they came at different times, Australian echoed through the house and the smell of Vegemite permeated the air. The tempo, in contrast to visitors who rushed to see the Hamilton Sculpture Gardens or Princeton University, was slower as both came with the aim of relaxing from their busy careers.

Abby's visit over Christmas meant we ate far too much. I received extra presents, including a squeaky snow-white rabbit to be affectionately known as Rabbitle. On Christmas Day, following an enormous lunch, we went into Princeton for a walk. The day was sunny but cold, so we all rugged up and walked the freshly cleared footpaths. I sniffed the generous bushes and trees while Mum and Abby gazed at the grand mansions that had graced the august grounds since Woodrow Wilson's time as the university's president.

Abby also let me sleep on the guest bed with her, and so I was sad when she left for a skiing trip in Canada. I was further flummoxed when Mum dashed away a couple of days later. It turned out that Ilana had broken her leg on Christmas Day, so Mum flew to Australia to play Florence Nightingale.

Making a speedy recovery, Ilana arrived a few months later. Her unusual visit consisted of perusing supermarket shelves for fat-free varieties of anything, or disappearing for hours to Mum's gym. The freezer filled with high-fibre and high-protein muffins and brownies, displacing the frozen chicken necks I loved.

On one rare gym-free day, Mum and Ilana took me for a constitutional along the neighbouring towpath that rose grandly like an island between the canal and nearby river. The idyllic summer scene could have been a forgery from a painting. Chatty Lycra-bedecked cyclists, lazy fishermen on portable seats, walkers in brightly coloured clothes, and boisterous dogs vied with us for the narrow pathway. I trotted along energetically, delighted to partake in this montage.

The arrival of red-and-blue plush towels embroidered with *Karen's B'nB* and *Chris's B'nB*, following another of Dalia's visits in late 2014, confirmed our five-star status. The Ritz-quality towels matched the generous shower caps, shampoos, conditioners and moisturisers on offer, liberated from our own hotel stays.

Our visitors hailed from the Australian cities of Brisbane, Perth, Melbourne, Sydney, Adelaide and Canberra, while United States locals travelled from San Francisco, Atlanta, Florida, Pittsburgh, Sea Girt and St Louis.

The St Louis contingent was also close family – Dad's brother Paul and his wife, Wendy. Paul sacrificed days of golf to make the visit, while Wendy, whose career as dog-minder made her a perfect companion, enlightened Mum about Paul and Dad's family history and produced shoe boxes full of photos.

Mum perfected menus for all tastes and seasons. Winter, of course, required cottage pie or baked chicken and biscuits. Within Mum's (dare I say rather limited) repertoire, these ensured raw mince – piquing nostalgic memories of the puppy treat of my childhood – or chicken titbits rewarded her trusty sous-chef. Had I been an American human, my gratitude journal would have contained daily thanks that my menu required no preparation other than opening a can or a packet of kibble.

More often than not, Dad took charge – grilling steaks on his fireplace BBQ, crunchy cobs of corn, slathered in butter with green beans 'for colour', as regular accompaniments.

His other mainstay was Bolognese sauce, served on pasta or spinach and ricotta pillows. Complementing any winter menu, freshly baked apricot, cherry or blueberry pie from the farm market up the road had a deceptive homemade appeal.

In summer, grilled Atlantic salmon and salad, or onion, garlic and sesame seed-laden bagels from the Bagel Barn near Mum's gym, topped with turkey, pastrami, smoked salmon, and egg and herring salad – all readily available from the Amish market or McAffrey's supermarket – were ideal. Mum's specialty – pavlova laden with passionfruit, kiwifruit and strawberries – ensured an Aussie theme, while for variety, key lime pie, thawed from its supermarket packaging, elicited groans of delight.

With all this experience, Mum and Dad flirted with the notion of opening as a paying proposition. But the vacancy rate that would be required to re-energise the hosts between guests would surely result in a loss-making proposition. It was agreed, therefore, that the Christmas tree harvest would have to fulfil the customer service quota – and the cash flow – required by this particular Australian and American family.

CHAPTER 18
A Tale of Two Tails

Rocky Hill, New Jersey
One blue-sky morning, summer heavily in the air, Mum took me for a walk in the gingerbread village of Rocky Hill, about 5 minutes from home. I leapt from the car, keen to investigate the concentrated smells emanating from a red fire hydrant. We then strolled along Route 508 past the post office. A picture-window travelshop and a hair salon, their entries paved with brightly coloured flower beds atop tangy mulch, were like flares for my attention.

But Mum was on a mission. When the footpath petered out, we climbed a higgledy-piggledy brick path and entered a pale pink doll's house.

As mixed aromas assailed me, I had the urge to lift my leg on a nearby wicker chair. The antiseptic odour of the shiny vinyl floor collided with fragrances wafting from an adjoining room. I looked up at Mum with baleful eyes – but she was unmoved. A discussion of suitable fur length in the draining heat ensued before I was unceremoniously abandoned into the care of my new stylist, Sue.

In Sydney, the normal practice had been for clients to

wander underfoot while awaiting their turn. Unfortunately here, as in Brisbane, I was caged in a rat-size crate instead. From this observation point, I was mesmerised by Sue, who was short, blonde and bubbly, with an infinite penchant for conversation. She wore heavy stage makeup and perform she did, her role being to style us as if we were about to model haute couture.

In a corner of the humid room into which Sue led me, a Schnauzer – neck extended, ears pricked and eyes alert – was almost submerged in a deep bath. On a high table in the centre of the room, a placid golden Cocker awaited his trim.

Ten crates were arranged around the walls. A couple of white Poodles huddled cosily, adjacent to me while a black-and-white Collie snored a few crates away. We adopted the lethargy that comes from a visit to the spa. Curling up to have a nap, I spied a Serena-like goddess opposite. With immaculate, long white-and-brown fur, a pink bow and a self-assured smirk, she was partly in the shade, so I hadn't noticed her initially. Memories of puppyhood humiliation rushed back and I imagined she was staring at me with contempt. I glowered at her from beneath shaded lids.

When it was my turn, Sue lathered me gently. Following this relaxing bath and a highly professional trim, blow dry and manicure, albeit with a continuous migraine-inducing commentary, we were taken out for a comfort stop – all of us except for this new 'Serena'. I wondered why she was confined inside, although she didn't object. I didn't have to wonder for long. When Mum returned, she was keen to be complimentary, while Sue, proud of her handiwork, took the opportunity to chat. Mum enquired about the ribbons, rosettes, certificates and newspaper articles adorning the walls.

'I have always shown dogs,' Sue explained. 'Coincidentally Penelope, my prize-winning Afghan Hound, is having her treatment today too. Penelope is famous – a regular competitor in the Westminster Dog Show.'

From Mum's hesitation, I realised the significance of this information was lost on her.

Undeterred, Sue elaborated. 'When Penelope isn't in a show, she stays next door in a carpeted salon. She can't run in the fields, play in the park or walk along the canal in case she's contaminated by dirt, bugs or other dogs.'

I was taken aback. Poor girl, this American Serena. It appeared her existence was only punctuated by competitions, during which she worked to win a ribbon or trophy, as had my parents. Determined to find out more about the show dog circuit when I returned to the salon, I hoped to gain some insight into the life I could have had, and no doubt that the real Serena was having, back in Australia.

But on my next visit a month later, I didn't see Penelope, though her scent travelled from the adjoining room. From discussions swirling about me, I learnt she annually enters in the prestigious Westminster Dog Show, where 2,500 dogs of up to 170 different breeds compete, though it was unclear whether she had actually won an award at this show.

Mum was as intrigued as I was – possibly wanting to find out more so she wouldn't be caught unaware again. Hitting the 'Westminster Kennel Club' website, she informed me that the Club was formed in 1877. Its bylaws stated that it aimed to 'increase the interest in dogs…and to hold an Annual Dog

Show in the City of New York'.

Now educated about dog shows to the equivalent of kindy level, Mum asked Sue if English Cockers attended.

'Indeed they do,' Sue said. 'Around a dozen or so regularly reach the finals. Some look like Sidnie, blue roans, but unlike Sidnie they all have their tails docked. And also unlike Sidnie,' she added with a wry smile, 'they are able to stand still – with their heads and tails up – for some time.'

Sue then returned to her preferred topic, boasting that Penelope had recently won an interstate dog show. Yet it seemed Penelope's reward for winning was more time in isolation, or occasionally in the treatment room, where unquestionably her regal superiority reigned.

I intended to overcome my shyness when my appointment next coincided with Penelope's grooming, aiming to raise the 'dog-show' topic with her. At last, my opportunity arose. As the other clients eavesdropped, occasionally opening one eye to observe or raising one ear to listen, I gulped and drew a deep breath. As humans tend to do, and given our standoffish introduction, I started with a positive observation, then something we had in common and, finally, a question about her life.

'Penelope, from your majestic posture I realise you must be a show dog. Coincidentally I come from a family of show dogs. My mother and father won many prizes, and some of my siblings were destined to compete. So I was wondering what you most enjoy about this life?'

Penelope stared at me as if considering whether she could believe the ancestry I claimed. Amazingly, deciding she could she said, 'It's a hard life as my goal is to win. The enjoyable part is when Sue gives me treats during the events and hugs and kisses after, but the rest of the time I'm pretty lonely.'

My eyes widened. My hugs and kisses arrived regularly and my life was anything but hard or lonely. If truth be told, everyone else's life revolved around mine. But her honesty allowed me to confess about my puppy shame.

'I was not attractive enough to be a show dog. My body is too long and my paws are too large. My sister Serena said I was only good enough to be a pet. But my life is wonderful, so why do I worry this might be somehow inferior?'

With a sage response, Penelope said, 'You are on a different path to your sister. One life is no better than the other. You should consider yourself fortunate. From stories I've heard at shows, some dogs have terrible lives and are treated badly. Some are even dumped by their owners.' Then, bored with our topic, she bluntly concluded, 'Just get over it.'

Getting over it was easy to do. I couldn't get excited about Penelope's career. The shows and isolation sounded tedious. If Sue was any warning, the owners took the competitions seriously, always having to display confidence, and the dogs needed to mimic this behaviour.

I felt sorry for these unlucky dogs. What was life without a romp outside to smell the critters? But mostly I was relieved to know that I was loved for being myself rather than for the competitions I might win. With a tinge of concern, I hoped that Serena's life in some way matched the joy I found in mine.

CHAPTER 19

The Pooch's P-rade

Princeton, 2014
Shortly after encountering a career show dog, I had my own taste of life in the public eye.

Warm weather in Princeton was celebratory. The Princeton University college year ended and reunions approached. As usual, Dad's college roommate Len and his wife, Sue, arrived from Atlanta to stay with us. Sue had beautiful thick red hair and a flawless peach complexion. A warm smile matched her innate generosity. A true gentleman, Len was gallant, compassionate and considerate of his wife and his friends. Having them as visitors was easy. They were comfortable with me and chatted amiably with my parents while I napped next to whoever joined me on the soft lounge.

Dad and Len had both attended Princeton University over fifty years ago and remained steadfast friends. Whenever possible they went to the reunion events together, filling the Memorial Day long weekend with the elation that properly kick-starts summer.

Princeton brings back alumni for a calendar-packed series of lectures, meals, dances and drinks, so that everyone reconnects and reminisces about the good old days. Five-year anniversaries are particularly significant, with alums firmly encouraged to attend and to donate generously. With 2014 being Dad and Len's fifty-fifth reunion, it was an important year.

Most significant on that reunion calendar was the Saturday afternoon fete: the 'P-rade'. Alums strutted proudly behind their class banners to the cheers of the following years' classes. Golf carts headed each delegation for those with walking difficulties. Every year, however, Dad procrastinated about participating in the P-rade. It was either too hot or too wet, to say nothing of too crowded or too long. But in 2014, as the weather was mild and sunny, he had no excuse.

Moreover, since I was the proud owner of an orange collar, leash and harness – the combo making a striking contrast to my black-and-white coat – Dad was chuffed to walk in the P-rade with a 'Princeton dog'.

We headed to the university's grounds and congregated at the shady 'Class of '59' gathering spot near the parade's start. I noticed other dogs milling around, but none as well attired. While they seemed friendly enough, the waiting crowd was large and oppressive. Barking my discomfort, I caught the attention of the Scottish band members engaged to accompany Dad's class. Their energetic rubs to my tummy briefly distracted me.

Finally, the first cart led off. Mum and I moved to the edge of the crowd to watch the procession. I was mesmerised by hundreds of pairs of feet. Leading the parade this year was the Class of '34 – a sole alum of over 100 years of age. He was not the only centenarian in the parade, however, with another from the next year following in quick succession, and then several nonagenarians and octogenarians.

When Dad's class took their turn at the head of the parade, Dad, Mum and I joined towards the rear, so I wasn't at risk of being crushed in the crowd. At around 77 years, Dad's mates were not so surefooted, and my weaving in and out of the throng could have tripped one up.

This was an important moment. I held my head high as I marched to the cheers, claps and waves of thousands of spectators. But once the scent of hot dogs drifted towards me, I veered closer to the crowd and began to think the afternoon could be more fun among the onlookers. Yet decked out in Princeton's colours and having received the honorific title from Dad's peers of 'class mascot', I focused on my duties. The whistles and applause made me think of the approbation Serena and Penelope received in their dog shows. I had a duty to uphold.

And what a duty it was. It was thirsty and tiring walking the length of the P-rade. After the two-hour march and constant attention, my head spun. I panted profusely and wearily dragged myself to the car.

I woke from my nap to hear Dad and Mum comment that now they had completed the P-rade, they didn't need to do that again. I agreed. This 'show' was not something I needed to repeat.

Perhaps I could finally relate in some small way to what my canine parents and Serena and Penelope had achieved in their lives. But in preference to dog shows, I'll take my peaceful walks in the fields any day!

CHAPTER 20

Where's Everyone Gone?

Princeton

By early July, the heat was oppressive. Every day mirrored the previous. Due to recent above-average rainfall, the Christmas trees and surrounding woods wore a deep green mantle, which could also become surprisingly crushing. Walls of trees bore down, reinforcing the claustrophobia from the heavy air. Grey and white mushrooms coated the fields, while only the late season, heat-baked ochre daffodils or deep orange lilies interrupted the dense bushes.

Of necessity we walked early in the morning or late in the afternoon – for a maximum of half an hour. My heart hammered and my long, pink tongue lolled out of my mouth. Returning to the house, I collapsed on any cool floor. Even the birds were too hot to sing. The middle of the day was cloaked in a weighty silence as people and animals alike sought shade and refuge.

A manifestation of this time struck me with surprise – everyone disappeared!

'Gone to the Shore' or 'Gone to Maine', as Bettie and Fred did annually, became the refrain. The only visitors were the tradesmen repainting and renovating the farmhouse in time for the friendly new tenants. As we viewed the farmhouse's rear stone yard across the expansive lawn from our deck, Mum admired the recent arrivals' overflowing pots of floral delights. And since I now reigned the entire property as canine-in-chief, invitations to drop in meant we could admire the couple's interior decorating skills, along with their expertise in gourmet dog-treat selection.

Annapolis, Maryland, June 2013
It soon appeared we would – at least for one year – follow the summer disappearance trend. Settled into my harness and safety belt in the car, I absorbed the paraphernalia surrounding me. My red-and-green tartan bed, my yellow towel, a large white mattress protector, my 'baby bone' and Christmas flea toys, were loaded onto the backseat. Why were they not in my bed spots inside?

After a couple of hours, we stopped at a small park somewhere in Pennsylvania to have lunch. I enjoyed water and a chicken-breast treat while Mum and Dad had cheese sandwiches, juice and cinnamon cakes, though they lamented the absence of coffee. Back in the car, we continued for a couple of hours. Lulled by the rolling wheels, I napped. Finally, we arrived at a mid-rise Annapolis hotel with canine scents lingering in the surrounding bushes, the foyer and the lift. Up five floors to our room, my bed and the mattress protector appeared. I congratulated America for its dog-welcoming practices and wished this arrangement could be copied in planes.

We enjoyed many outings during this summer spell. Since it was before our first Thanksgiving visit to Aunt Lucie's, I thoroughly investigated the house and yard, and sniffed out the cats inside and the squirrels hiding in the garden.

Downtown, we strolled along the narrow, congested streets near the port. The whole town was happy and relaxed. I was patted by strangers and given water to combat the heat. Mum, Dad and Lucie ate meals non-stop, enjoying a particularly tasty Thai extravaganza, while I rested in shady spaces.

At night, we returned to our hotel, where I was vigilant at providing security, barking at hallway intruders and at the repeated banging of doors. Our first night was particularly unsettled as a large number of wedding guests returned from their celebrations. Eventually I gave up trying to outperform the baby crying in the adjoining room and fell asleep. Thankfully our second night was quieter.

Princeton, July 2013
A week or so after we returned from this vacation, on a warm early July evening, a white car pulled into our driveway. I had been uneasy for several days as I noticed Mum's increasing tension, coupled with her having barely unpacked before she began repacking. With bags lined up at the door, instead of us all bundling into our car together again, Mum kissed Dad and me and settled herself in the stranger's car. As they pulled away, Dad and I were left awkwardly and abruptly alone. With a feeling like a bowling ball had landed in the pit of my stomach, I turned and walked back into the house just with Dad, as the last light of day ebbed.

Mum's disappearance at this time of year to our homeland became a regular stint, leaving us boys to fend for ourselves. It took time for me to adjust. While she was away, life became less formal, though. Mealtimes were punctual and walks continued. But more often than not, rather than foraging in the fields, we visited Bettie for ice cubes and a pick-up chat – before she and Fred similarly took off.

As Mum left just after the July fourth fireworks, I responded to these thereafter with trepidation at her impending absence, as well as annoyance at the rat-a-tat explosions that had me barking for hours. Amusing in hindsight, the first time we heard sounds like gunshots, Dad called the police. Mum and I hid in the bedroom, certain we were being burgled. The exasperated police officer, who arrived within minutes of Dad's call, soundly ticked him off for crying wolf.

Mum's trips home to Oz lasted three weeks. For the majority of the American population who abscond at this time of year, stays of two to three months, as far north or east to the beach as possible, were customary. But since we'd lived 10 minutes from world-famous Bondi Beach in Sydney, day trips to beachside Sea Girt where Dad's glider-pilot stepson and his jovial, musical partner, Annie, had a summer home, sufficed.

★ ★ ★ ★

Sea Girt, New Jersey
Annie was a lot of fun, full of energy and a great cook. Pete regaled us with his brave hang-gliding ventures, from traversing sparse deserts to crossing deep canyons. Recently his career had transformed into flying dogs and cats from the

south, left homeless by hurricanes and floods, up north to new owners.

The rellies (Aussie for relatives) always ensured that the invitation to Sea Girt for lunch explicitly included me, although it meant their two striking and adored Siamese cats had to be confined to the back bedroom. One short exposure, at which I reacted as expected – bounding at the terrified animals – curtailed future viewings. I demonstrated my appreciation by cleaning up any leftovers in the cats' bowls. I also welcomed being free to roam during lunch, so I could scour the kitchen or scout around under the dining table.

To ensure no accidents inside, we took at least two walks to the beach, a couple of blocks away, although dogs weren't allowed on the boardwalk in summer. Nevertheless, with many resident or visiting dogs in Sea Girt, the sidewalks always reeked of interesting dog scents for me to stop and smell. While I did this, Mum and Annie admired the flower gardens and the veggie and herb beds. Annie was the fount of all wisdom in relation to plants suitable for each season, but regardless of Abby's going-away present to Mum of a book titled *Growing Vegetables,* Mum would not find her green fingers until several years later. Not even the supposedly hardy 'mums she planted two falls ago bloomed.

Annie's other claim to fame was her proficiency playing the harp and piano. She took a small harp to Sea Girt from their home in Pittsburgh, where her career involved giving piano lessons to children. In Sea Girt, she entertained the neighbours' children on the shady front porch in the early morning or late afternoon.

I fell asleep, a full tummy and a walk in the sea air

combining to wipe out this totally content four-legged guest – always keen for the next dependable invite to the Shore.

...   *

Portland, Maine
In stark contrast to the welcome mat's repeated airings in Sea Girt, no such offer was to follow our one and only jaunt to Fred and Bettie's lakeside cabin in Maine. An extended trip, it had to be planned with military precision, with advance bookings in dog-friendly lodgings along our way. A typical rustic cabin, set high to capture the water views, greeted us when we arrived in Portland, licking our lips in anticipation of fresh lobster. We were excited at the thought of seeing first-hand their kayaking, canoeing and fishing by-the-lake jewel.

Seated around a square wooden table, about to hoe into the day's moist catch, I detected a movement out of the corner of my eye. With a flash, I bounded after one of the cats who had dared peep down from the safety of the loft. Standing lamps crashing, furniture toppling and cat screeching, it deftly avoided my lunges, its escape route hard-wired into its GPS. Sadly, the next year when Fred, Bettie and the cats headed to Maine, we were demoted to taking in their mail and watering the plants – activities of servitude, rather than of being served!

CHAPTER 21

The Third Dimension

Princeton
Our family vacations provided companionship and comfort for us all. I was reminded of how I'd won the jackpot with my parents. Bringing this home to me with a solid punch in the guts was an unexpected and unnerving experience.

On hot summer mornings, I woke with the sun. I jumped up on Mum's side of the bed to let her know I was ready for breakfast. Occasionally she shushed me back to sleep, or I scampered downstairs to relieve myself and see if there were any critters around to bark at, thus achieving the same goal of waking the caterers.

One morning when my bladder propelled me out my doggie door prior to summoning breakfast service, I was surprised to see a black-and-white Pit Bull in our driveway. The large solid dog looked towards the road but barked yelp for yelp as I similarly expressed my outrage at its trespassing on our property.

Two different barks reverberating around the front yard had the desired effect. Mum flew downstairs to see the cause of the commotion. Trapped between her angst at finding an animal in distress and her anxiety at approaching an unknown dog of this breed, she agonised over why it was here, whether it was hungry or thirsty, and what she should do.

For me, with breakfast now moments away and, bored with this scene, I ate and promptly went back to sleep for my morning beauty nap.

My departure quietened our intruder, who moved towards the farmhouse – from which direction, we later learnt, he had initially arrived. Our new farmhouse tenants called Animal Control to collect the dog – but then it disappeared. Uneasy, Mum drove around the neighbourhood hoping to confirm the dog had indeed left our property before we went for a walk. With no sighting on the nearby roads, Mum cautiously deemed the coast clear. She returned and we headed off towards the Christmas tree fields via the backyard and past the swimming pool.

To Mum's horror, the dog suddenly appeared on the far side of the back bridge, barking and growling at us, now in its direct line of sight.

It began to cross the bridge.

Mum yanked me around and made a hasty, yet controlled, dash back towards my fenced-in yard. As we neared, she screamed for Dad.

The dog continued to bark, growl and approach, but thankfully not at a pace that would outrun us. I hadn't had the wits about me to warn the dog off, but as Mum's shaking and screams coursed through me, bewilderment, fear and finally anger at my walk being curtailed, now converged. Mum shook as she recounted the incident to Dad, who hadn't heard her screams due to the double glazing on the windows. She thanked her lucky stars she hadn't taken a different path for our walk. Had we walked to the bridge from the fields rather than the house, we would have had no quick, unimpeded escape. Mum called Animal Control again and a couple of hours later an officer arrived. He approached the dog from the same route we had, but stopped short when confronted with its aggressive growling. He said we were fortunate it had wanted to protect its chosen hideout rather than give chase. In truth, it could easily have outrun us.

The officer assembled a wire cage-like trap and left its end open. He put treats inside, assuming the dog had been dumped the previous night and was now ravenous. Hours passed but still the dog stubbornly remained under the back bridge for protection and shade. We couldn't go for a walk and Dad couldn't groom the fields. We were prisoners. I grew fidgety. The atmosphere tensed. Mum alternated between shock and relief at our close call.

With no movement by mid-afternoon, two officers from Animal Control returned with a plan. They alternated between good cop – the lady holding a delectable sausage – and bad cop – the man armed with the long stick with a noose at the end. Unimpressed with their armory, I retreated to bed once more, hackles raised, in case they came near me.

With patience and gentle coaxing, the probably now-starving dog emerged from its hiding spot. It rushed forward to get some food and then darted back to the safety of the bridge. It repeated this behavior until it took a moment to pee. The officer with the noose swooped, trapping the dog by its neck. Mournful sounds propelled me from my bed. Wide-eyed, we watched as the poor dog was dragged into the van, in which a cage had been prepared. The stray, as everyone now referred to it, quietened, looking less fearful than it had the entire day.

The empathetic lady officer explained he would be held for a week in case his owner was found or came forward. She added that was unlikely, as Pit Bulls are rarely microchipped; he was probably dumped as he was unmanageable. Eventually they would determine if he could be rehabilitated as a rescue dog.

We were all downcast after this experience. Mum and Dad wandered around aimlessly. My ears drooped, my tummy churned and my tail hung. I had selfishly thought of myself as a fallen show dog who had landed on his feet as a loved and pampered pet. I had never contemplated such a different life – one of constant fear of being hurt or dumped by my owner, uncertain about the prospect of being rescued. According to The Last Resort Animal Rescue and Wildlife Refuge in New Jersey, four million dogs and cats are euthanised in the US each year.

For many of us there are alternative lives too horrible to consider, even as numerous organisations make it their purpose to address these injustices. In the States, Best Friends, The Humane Society and the American Society for the Prevention of Cruelty to Animals exist, to which Mum generously contributed when we were there. In Australia, The Royal Society for the Prevention of Cruelty to Animals is what Mum refers to as 'my charity', having made them the major recipient of her donations.

No wonder blessed dogs like me return deep love and loyalty to our precious caring owners.

Part Eight
The Departure

CHAPTER 22

Ambassador's Reign Reined

Princeton, October 2014
Australia's support of US foreign policy is appreciated by American politicians and acknowledged by much of the public. And when Americans undertake the 15-hour plus flight to visit our country, they glowingly describe its natural beauty and the approachability and humour of Aussies like us.

As ambassadors to the States, we were welcomed with open arms. In return, we were on our best behaviour, except where stark cultural differences warranted exposure. In those instances, Mum and I have been allowed to speak our minds, and while not citizens, we exercised the First Amendment right as if we were. So, it was with regret that my American adventure had to be prematurely curtailed after two and a half years – as a result, I must note, of Mum's Homeland Security 'advice'.

'If you listen to me,' the burly Customs agent cautioned her when the short Italian holiday she'd taken with Dad resulted in the possibility she would be denied readmission to the States, 'spend more time in your home country in contrast to your brief visits.'

Presumably he feared that Mum sought to become a permanent resident – the last thing on her mind with both her children and property in Australia. His personal fear or not, her own fears mounted. Would any fleeting trip outside the States be interpreted as a means to re-enter the country for another extended period?

She acted accordingly. Plans commenced for us both to return home – in my case permanently. For Mum it meant at least six months in Australia with only short return trips to the States until Australia became Mum and Dad's main base.

In truth, the time was right for me to undertake the long return trip. I was ageing – gracefully but undeniably. Black patches were flecked with grey, and white fur was now speckled. My ears had morphed from black to dark grey, and my eyebrows could have done with a tint. I also had some lumps and bumps that my vet considered 'normal for a man of my age'. At eight and a half years, my energy waxed and waned. My patience was short. I barked often and I barked early – first thing in the morning, approaching dinner and when my routine wasn't followed to the letter. Blueberries follow breakfast; a tablet in a pill pocket follows dinner, even if the pill pocket is empty and the tablet unnecessary; lunch is served when the parents have theirs; an evening treat is mandatory; and a nap follows meals.

Mum and Dad thankfully had also reached the age of routine. Their eating and sleeping regimes matched my own, and we were all done with partying.

But for a dog to enter Australia entailed what the US Department of Agriculture referred to as an 'arduous' process – Australian citizen or not. Admission to the States required a rabies shot and an expensive ticket. Admission to Australia involved an encyclopaedia of procedures, although the steep ticket cost was consistent.

The first step in transporting a dog into Australia from the States necessitated intensive scrutiny of the Department of Agriculture's website. The good news was that quarantine in Australia had been reduced from one month to ten days. The bad news was that Stateside preparation was a minimum of six months prior to 'export'.

Action swirled around me, working back from my spring departure, thus avoiding flights in extreme hot or cold weather. A rabies shot and blood test initiated the timetable. The treatments that followed involved two flu shots, further blood tests for unpronounceable diseases, and internal and external parasite tablets.

The paperwork and fees cost more than a business-class ticket and included the rabies certificate and fee, the Import Permit Application and fee, the Export Agent engagement and cost, the flight fee, and the quarantine application and fee. The pedantic documentation, administration and tracking were to verify my identity and confirm I had been decontaminated as required to return to the island that is rabies-free Australia.

Mum organised everyone. Her supervision included Dad, who would be responsible for the final procedures as Mum would leave for Australia a month before me; the vet who duly followed Mum's extensive checklists; and the export agent who was interrogated and monitored from go to whoa.

After two and a half years in absentia, my transportation crate, the mini-RV, reared its ugly head again and became the new piece of main bedroom furniture. With the approach of Mum's departure, the tension crackled. Dad and I walked on eggshells, and even my codger-like behaviour had to be curtailed in the interests of peace.

Finally the day arrived. One moment Mum was there and the next moment Dad was driving her away, the Jeep laden with every ounce of her allowable luggage limit. I stared longingly down the drive, following my bath of kisses and promises for our speedy reunion on the other side of the world.

Princeton, April 2015
A different quiet prevailed. The empty house felt like part of its spirit had vacated. Dad felt it too. He walked from room to room and looked around. He patted me and sighed. The whirlwind no longer blew, and our indoor activities were concentrated in the only rooms two batching boys needed – the kitchen, our bedroom and Dad's study.

We perked up when Mum called to tell us of her safe arrival. Dad diligently completed my further few weeks of pre-departure activities and kept our bodies together. We ate, drank, slept and continued my daily two-walk routine. Occasionally I would humour the old man and sleep in the crate.

Déjà-vu thundered back thick and fast when a van arrived, and in I went. But as I glanced at Dad through my mesh door, my heart didn't race. I remembered Mum's words. I was on my way to our promised reunion.

Part Nine
After

CHAPTER 23
The Re-entry

Eastern Creek, New South Wales, April 2015
A seasoned air traveller, I took my flight west to LAX in my stride. With mild weather, the trip was uneventful. My long-haul departure was not as tranquil as my arrival via San Francisco, but, thanks to Mum and her team, my requisite Customs and Security documentation had been completed 'to the letter', so there were no hiccups. After a night and long day in the massive airport with scores of barking and whining fellow travellers, I was winging my way home.

My flight into Sydney was rough. Bumps and buffeting increased the longer we flew. My numerous companions alternated between overwhelming silence and bursts of ear-splitting horror, but as we had left the US late at night, my beauty-sleep needs predominated. My stress levels rose, however, with our descent. Severe turbulence from drenching rains and gale force winds had us all in panic mode. My crate wobbled forward as we touched down, but soon we were rolling across the tarmac as smoothly as if I was back in our Jeep.

My ears promptly unblocked – a sign that I now associated

with my exit. As I was moved down the ramp and onto another snaking trolley, the torrential downpour marking our Sydney entry sounded like nails being hammered on the roof of my crate. For during this autumn, the east coast of Australia featured floods from the day I landed to the day I was freed from quarantine, a particularly unpleasant stay as my resort accommodated guests in runs, partly open to the sodden skies.

But before we left the airport for this one-star hotel, we awaited other international flights carrying dogs who would be boarding with me. At last, a group of frenzied, hungry hounds were loaded into a van. A cacophony of barking in different languages provided a constant backdrop until I laid eyes on Mum again.

I wasn't to know, but Mum was also out that day in the teeming rain. Her objective was to deliver my special food to the Eastern Creek Quarantine Station, a trip possibly worse than mine. She navigated flooded Sydney roads and queues of cars on a journey that would normally take an hour but took her double that time. Yet her mission of mercy worked. Awaiting me when we were finally served dinner were both my dietary food and my eye ointment, though after one dose, it became apparent that room service considered my ointment application non-essential. Ten dreary, wet and cold days followed. The dampness and mouldy smell increased.

One morning, with the sun's reappearance, several of us were loaded into our crates again and moved to an open but covered concrete area. Peering from a doorway was a sea of new faces. I jumped with joy when I recognised one of those smiles – my mum's!

I barked and barked until it was my turn to be released. Hugging and kissing as we made a quick escape, Mum happily donated the crate to the hotel for future use – neither of us having any wish to see it again.

My stress dissipated immediately and I curled up on the front seat of Mum's car. She constantly reached out to caress me, despite my soggy aroma. Springing into action, she called our local groomers. Yes, they could fit in an overseas traveller that afternoon. A luxurious bath ensued.

Vaucluse, from April 2015
At almost nine years, I now had another wonderful period ahead of me. Mum was retired, and we were back in our home country and our home, wrapped in the ethos we were brought up in and understood.

The next three years passed enjoyably as we resettled in Vaucluse. Dad travelled to the States for a few months in spring and winter to tend to his Christmas trees and oversee the harvest, and Mum joined him for several weeks twice a year. I stayed home with my beds, toys and food, my vet and grooming amenities nearby as Maggie, my (new) warm, happy and fit dogsitter, moved in to take care of me. Her life revolved around me, so my every need was accommodated. Mum always returned with an American pressie of a fluffy toy – my pink kangaroo becoming a patriotic favourite, seconded by a unique red-and-blue Navajo Indian patterned jumper that could only be an American fashion statement.

Our routine snapped back to normal – a walk around Vaucluse village every morning, whether before or after

Mum's gym session; a stop at Nino's for coffee and pats. Morning tea and dried chicken-breast fillet treats from our local vet often followed, then tuna and apple for lunch. Next came a nap while Mum shopped or read, capped off with an afternoon walk. These days were perfection.

I even tolerated short doggie dates with my cousins Murphy and Diego. We visited Ilana and Mark at their Newtown terrace house on Saturday afternoons, where we dogs jostled for lap space. Diego and I curled up on Mum or Ilana's lap in front of the gas fire that burned regardless of the season. Solid and large, Murphy only managed to put his front paws up on the couch or a lap, until he realised it was fruitless and lay down at Mark's feet.

One neighbour I loved to visit was Suellen, who lived with her Cavalier King Charles Spaniels Louie and Molly a few homes along the street from ours. We regularly dropped in, particularly when Mum was away, as Suellen and Maggie were good friends. I always checked their food bowls – unfortunately usually empty. Sometimes we watched Suellen, Louie and Molly play 'fetch' at Christison Park. I had never mastered this art and couldn't understand their conscientious focus on the bright orange ball. Instead, I preferred to veer towards the wetlands and their birdlife directly in front of South Head Lighthouse.

I never tired of the sameness of our walks around the sloping streets near home. Occasionally we took a longer course, descending the S-bends that led to the city. We'd sometimes hop off this route to climb steep Towns Road towards Rose Bay North shopping centre, my destination of choice being the deli, a favourite coffee stop of Maggie's, where the delightful South African owners rewarded me with treats of biltong.

A regular, though now domestic, holiday for Mum and me was visiting Abby in Canberra, where she had moved on returning from England. We stayed in her cosy house where normal rules relaxed, and I slept on her bed with her or on the futon with Mum.

Between predictable times at home with Mum and Dad or Maggie and holidays in Canberra, this period of my life back in Australia was only to improve on the one paw, while commencing a period tinged with sadness and inevitability on another.

CHAPTER 24

An Aussie Horse Farm

Outside Canberra, from February 2018
A few months shy of my twelfth birthday, two significant events unfolded.

The first revolved around Abby's desire to own a horse. Abby's career based in Australia's capital Canberra had the benefit of allowing her to keep a horse close to where she lived. She purchased an Arabian mare called Tallah. For several years, Tallah was agisted near Abby's home on the fringes of Canberra, which meant that morning and evening feeds were easily manageable.

Abby spent her weekends riding around the nearby vineyards, attending jumping clinics and competing in dressage, show jumping and cross-country events. As her skills improved, her dream was to live on a farm with Tallah, within commuting distance from work.

Mum and Dad were enlisted in the search. Locations around the towns of Gundaroo, Murrumbateman and Yass, around 45 minutes from Canberra, were considered. While they all agreed it would take a year to find the right property, when the Waldmans decide on a plan, proceedings invariably accelerate. With Abby's weeks full of horse-riding events, ice-hockey competitions and, of course, work, she was happy to delegate. Mum, Dad and I often led the charge, inspecting properties to see if they should be culled or classified: 'has potential'.

A property we viewed in early 2018 was idyllic. Its landscape was pocked with worn prehistoric boulders, whose colours varied from green to grey to rust depending on the light. Eucalyptus, wattle and oak trees ranged over the 9 spacious hectares, while its elevated position extended the typically Australian bushland vista towards the Brindabellas. Being high summer, the fields wore a dusty dry coat, though the irrigated yard extending around three sides of the house was lush. The three-tiered bird bath adorning the entry garden attracted green, yellow and red parakeets; grey, pink and white parrots; bright blue wrens; tiny finches; and even the magpie family that called this property home.

Mum thought the house was perfect, its five bedrooms providing ample space for Abby to have a luxurious bedroom, study and even a gym, with a separate bedroom at the other end of the house for Mum, Dad and me – plus a guest room for family and friends to stay over. I loved the garden, huge compared to my Sydney yard, with its panoramic view of horses on the property and smelling of nearby kangaroos, rabbits and echidnas.

With Abby's criterion of horse infrastructure also achieved – with six well-fenced paddocks, an arena, a huge shed, a dam and even a bore – the deal was sealed.

Domestic holidays now became bucolic visits to the Aussie farm. We stayed for weeks at a time, gradually upgrading the roads, fencing, arena, water supply and heating.

Abundant couches provided perfect sleeping pads during the day when I wasn't exploring the terraced gardens surrounding the enormous grass yard. I supervised Tallah and Abby's friends' horses in the paddocks and snacked on the cartilage littering the gravel after the horses had been shod.

For almost two years we regularly travelled the Hume Highway between Sydney and the farm, a three-and-a-half-hour trip. Sometimes we interrupted our journey with brunch at a café in Berrima in the Southern Highlands. As I sat politely on Mum's old brown coat, I had my kibble morning tea while Mum and Dad shared thick ricotta hotcakes oozing with maple syrup.

More often than not, we stopped at our friends Edith and Frank's new home in Bowral, on the opposite side of the railway from where I'd been born. The wooded property was lined with beds of orchids, roses and lilies that epitomised Edith's green fingers. After sharing dry chicken breast fillets with Sassa and Zephy, their mini-Schnauzers, we hovered under the dining table as our parents chatted and enjoyed Edith's spread. Her servings of smoked salmon, egg salad, tangy herring salad, Hungarian cream cheese with paprika and spicy salami on dense rye with strong espresso and slabs of bon vivant were well renowned.

At the farm, a regular parade of visitors arrived from Sydney or the South Coast. I was duly spoilt with walks around the property or afternoons lounging in front of the fire. Life was relaxed and took on a more laid-back pace than in Sydney. But of course, as I'd learnt before, life always confronts us with unexpected challenges.

CHAPTER 25

Gentle Latter Years

Sydney, from February 2018

Not long after contracts had been exchanged on the farm, my world began to wobble. It started during a regular check-up at our local Vaucluse vet. Discretion requiring dearth of detail, suffice it to say that we boys need our anal sacs flushed from time to time. On one of these unpleasant occasions, our caring and conscientious vet Julie found a small lump where it shouldn't have been.

Events moved quickly. The following day I had an appointment with a disarming and empathetic surgeon in Sydney's North Shore. Subjected to a battery of blood tests, CT scans and an ultrasound, my diagnosis was confirmed. I had a cancerous lump.

Surgery was scheduled. Reasonably successful, the lump and several lymph nodes were excised, but Mum and Dad were advised that cancer cells would still be floating around. Chemotherapy, giving me a twelve to eighteen-month prognosis, was recommended, reasonably unobtrusive in that it could be given in tablet form, with minimal, if any, side effects. Mum and Dad made clear to the oncologist that my quality of life was their main priority. If chemo and supplementary medication didn't detract from my walks and my appetite that was fine, but I would not be subjected to radical or heroic experiments that made me sicker than the cancer.

We had to work through two physicians prior to landing on the cancer expert who stayed with us throughout my illness. The first doctor left the practice, and the second young woman had to constantly check with colleagues until she thankfully fell off our radar. Finally, an experienced doctor took over and gave the three of us confidence in his availability and expertise.

I barely felt any side effects from the treatment for about eighteen months. The rare moments of elevated liver function were managed. Mum inserted the little blue and orange chemo tablets into slices of banana or sliced chicken, so they became dessert for me three times a week. Mum and Dad continued shortened trips to the States. Maggie looked after my medication and life continued as I'd always enjoyed. Mum's desperate angst and teary outbursts receded, Mum finally finding her gardening prowess in the farm's backyard, and we both enjoyed our life together.

But at just over thirteen years, I began to require additional amelioration. Tablets to lower calcium levels. Tablets for bouts of nausea. Tablets for ongoing diarrhea. Coupled with my unabated eye and ear treatments, as well as the occasional dose of antibiotics, my increasingly confusing wellness program required a spreadsheet so Mum and Maggie could keep track.

This regime took its toll, and my condition deteriorated.

Things became dire while Mum and Dad were holidaying in Spain and Portugal in June 2019. Changing her flights back to Australia twice, Mum flew home three weeks early.

She then nursed me back to whatever full health is for a dog with cancer. For the next eight months, life again became peaceful. We continued to visit the farm, but there were no more overseas trips for Mum. Dad went to the States alone for a shortened stay, fortunately returning in late 2019 in time for us to gather at the farm. With a ferocious bush fire season soon at hand, Mum wanted to be at the ready if Abby needed support.

As fires continued to rage across New South Wales, we still needed to go back to Sydney for my specialist visits, alas with increasing frequency. My appetite varied, so Mum adjusted my diet to whatever I fancied. After years of being given a careful diet, I was now indulged with treats no man or beast could resist – Mum's homemade chicken soup with boiled chicken, grilled John Dory, canned tuna, sardines, slices of apple, pear and banana, and even ricotta or cottage cheese mixed with Weet Bix. But, after initially devouring it all with gusto, I slowly lost interest in my meals. It was impossible to continue with my chemo as the tablets caused aggravated bouts of colitis and diarrhea. The cancer spread and my calcium levels rose. I was continually thirsty and panted profusely.

By early March 2020, I wanted most to sleep, rewarding Mum for her steadfast devotion with an occasional walk. To make her happy, I sporadically tolerated spoonfuls of chicken soup or mouthfuls of John Dory. We returned to Sydney to see the specialist.

Strong words from my doctor made it clear that it was time to face what Mum had dreaded. I didn't mind. Instead of the twelve to eighteen months I had been promised, I'd enjoyed two years of happiness and serenity. Having learnt with Sapta, Mum knew to tell me she could release me.

Caring Julie and nurse Chelsy provided my needed relief at home. My last moments were spent cuddled in Mum's arms. She kissed my head over and over as Dad watched on sadly. I slipped away just before 3pm on 11 March 2020.

With the Coronavirus pandemic immediately thereafter sweeping through the world, at least Mum and Dad wouldn't have to seek emergency medical help for me in those trying times. They isolated with Abby at the farm, giving solace to each other as they and the world at large mourned those lost. And fought to celebrate life.

Afterword

Following a long period of Writer's Block beginning with Sidnie's cancer diagnosis, I was able to write again about his life only after Sidnie passed away.

With the heartbreak and devastation of the coronavirus pandemic at the forefront of mind every day, Sidnie's story reminds us to luxuriate in the pleasures and adventures to be found at home and nearby, and to revere the companionship and comfort provided by our wonderful four-legged friends.

Out of my profound heartbreak and deep grief, I hope to express his uniqueness, and to honour his love and loyalty, by sharing my memories of Sidnie with others who have similarly loved a dog with every fibre of their being.

My wish is that you enjoy getting to know my Sidnie – so truly special to me.

Regrettably, Sidnie's cousin Diego and friends Parker, Maya, Boston and Sassa have also now passed away. I know their parents similarly grieve deeply for them. I wish Sidnie and Diego and Sidnie's mates have all reunited for a happy romp together.

For me, my Sidnie will remain forever in my heart.

Karen Waldman
17 January 2022

Acknowledgements

As narrator, I am grateful to a few special people for their assistance in writing this book.

My editor from early days, Catherine Adams of Inkslinger Editing, New York, was always cheerful, positive and ready to give me constructive suggestions and advice that enriched Sidnie's adventures, humour and voice.

The book couldn't have come to fruition without the professional management of Bernadette Foley of Broadcast Books, Sydney. Always thoughtful and pragmatic, she steered Sidnie's manuscript through the mysterious publishing processes.

To my daughters, Ilana and Abby, I thank you wholeheartedly for being gentle supporters of my new career, keen commentators along the way, and indispensable technology gurus.

My husband Chris patiently read draft after draft, providing valuable comment and input and, as a dual national, timely insights into the American psyche, while quietly clapping my endeavours and loudly encouraging my progress.

I'm sure I could not have continued this project through its eight-year gestation without all their support and love.

www.ingramcontent.com/pod-product-compliance
Lightning Source LLC
Chambersburg PA
CBHW041501010526
44107CB00049B/1610